The Money Fountain

CREATING WEALTH, GROWING WEALTH MADE SIMPLE

Robert J Van Eyden
and
P D Wells

The Money Fountain

Self-published—Robert J Van Eyden
www.themoneyfountain.com
info@themoneyfountain.com

ISBN-10: 1492812099
ISBN-13: 978-1492812098
Library of Congress Control Number: 2013919474
CreateSpace Independent Publishing Platform
North Charleston, South Carolina

Graphic design and layout by CreateSpace

This book is dedicated to my wife, Renee, my son, Ethan, and my sister Michelle.
The northern stars in my life

"Do not be held by what has been done before, but instead by what is possible."

—*Elon Musk*

CHAPTER 1
DESTINY

As the seasons changed, the land became a kaleidoscope of colours. During winter, the sprouting wheat turned the rolling hills into a sea of jade, and as the months slipped by, the ripening wheat transformed the landscape into an ocean of gold. After the harvest, the summer sun burnt the soil a deep sienna. Then the earth waited for winter's soft rains to inspire the cycle of life again.

Mr February called this abundance.

As he grew up, Ash would come to know a different kind of abundance, but he started out very small. He entered life on a mission station, hidden in the rolling wheat fields of southern Africa. His home was a modest two-bedroom house on a dusty street. He shared this space with his parents, two brothers, a sister, and his grandfather, Mr February.

Though money was scarce, there was a roof over their heads and food on the table. Their home was often filled with love and laughter, but Ash's father had a weakness for alcohol, and when he hit the bottle he would vent his frustration violently. During these episodes, Ash fled into the wheat lands, where he spent hours watching the wind dance across the fields. He was fascinated by the way it candidly changed direction. Sometimes it seemed to wait, then it would dart away in any direction it chose. This wind was always light and free and seemed to laugh in delight. Ash aspired to be like this wind.

In a small way, fortune smiled on the family's poverty. Mr February was a carpenter, and it was he who kept the wolf from the door. He was honest and reliable and worked hard. He always delivered more than was expected, and this kept his customers coming back. Mr February was the person who opened the first door in Ash's life. He sent him to school, and it was here that Ash found rugby.

Ash enjoyed the challenge of this physical contact sport. He was faster than the other boys, and he ran like the wind dancing over the wheat fields. He ran with humour, teasing and taunting his opponents. Sometimes he ran backwards, away from the advancing team, but he always turned and ran at them jinking, weaving, gliding, and laughing. He scored often and celebrated each touchdown with his trademark cartwheel display, which ended with an enthusiastic bound into the air. Then, smiling, he trotted back to join his teammates. His supporters loved him, and their cheers spurred him to greater heights.

When he was fifteen, he was selected to play in the first team, and whenever the team played at home, the whole community turned out to watch. They arrived early to claim the best seats and brought picnic hampers, which they enjoyed before the match started. In a carnival atmosphere, the tension grew as kick-off drew near, and when the players took to the field, the crowd left no doubt as to whom they had come to support.

Thanks largely to Ash's efforts, the team won the league, and on this day, his fans carried him through the streets on their shoulders chanting his name. He was their lucky star, a celebration of their potential.

Young love also found its way into Ash's life. He had his eye on Suraya, the prettiest girl in the village. She had also noticed him and cautiously welcomed his advances. By and by, she grew to trust him and allowed him closer. One full moon, out in the wheat fields, their young love was sealed with a kiss. His cup of joy overflowed.

When Ash looked back on his life, he called these days spent in the wheat fields his days of abundance. He wished they would never end, but youth is a fleeting visitor. Destiny had other plans for him.

His career took another leap when he was selected to represent the provincial under-nineteen rugby team. This was his chance to fly and he grasped it with both hands. Even though the competition in this league was tougher, it allowed him to display his talents, and he excelled. The crowds were bigger and they loved Ash, who grew addicted to their roar. As the applause lifted him up, he felt a new power surge through his legs, as if he were flying. Once again, Ash had a big hand in bringing the trophy home, and when the tournament ended, Ash was voted best player.

Senior provincial scouts sought Ash out and offered him large sums of money and contracts with attractive benefits. Such was the interest in his talent, the scouts competed to outbid each other. The baited hook was dangled enticingly before him. Ash began drifting away from Mr February's abundance, towards a new abundance he didn't understand.

Mr February had advised him wisely. "Stay close to home, where you know who you are. Greedy people will set traps for you, and you will not see these traps."

But Ash knew better. He wanted to soar with the eagles and test his skills against the best. The lure of glory seduced him. He was attracted by the promise of the big smoke, the bright lights, money, fame, and glory. Self-importance and vanity now became regular visitors in Ash's life.

After due consideration, Ash accepted the best contract with the richest team—the Johannesburg-based Lions. He went to Egoli, the city of gold. On the field he excelled and the crowds loved him; but they loved him too much. Ash was a small-town boy in a big pond filled with big fish, and sirens. He had grown up in a village where people meant what they said, and he assumed that everybody was like that. He had heard talk of gold-diggers and fair-weather friends but didn't know any. He liked his new friends, and they made him feel good. Gradually, Ash began to believe that he was ten feet tall and made of steel.

The night Mr February passed away Ash dreamt that he was drifting in a shark-infested sea. Had he been older and wiser, he would have realised that these were not sharks but troubles of his own making that had come to find him.

Ash had always had a nagging feeling that he was being observed. He sensed a presence but could not identify it. Sometimes this presence fell behind, but it always caught up. Occasionally, it seemed to present opportunities, and sometimes he had lucky escapes. Sometimes it seemed to Ash as if his destiny was sucking him towards a fate over which he did not seem to have much control.

In his new home in the City of Gold, Ash's sporting career bloomed, and soon he was called up for the national squad, the famed and feared Springbok Rugby Team. Once again, he excelled, and it did not take long before he stamped his name on his position and the number 14 jersey became his. The crowds were bigger and their roar was thunderous. They loved Ash, and when he took the field, it was as if he and the wind were one. In this super league, he teamed up with Bobby, who had the knack of attracting three defenders and was still able to deliver the "pop ball" into Ash's hands. Given the space, the fleet-footed Ash wove his magic. On occasion, for the sheer joy of running, he pinned his ears back and beat his opponents with pure speed. Each touchdown was followed by his cartwheeling celebration. The crowds adored their new hero, and he played to them.

But Ash became overconfident, and this bloomed into arrogance. He began to think he was better than others. Just as destiny had feared, Ash was swallowed by the good times—flashy cars, parties, and women. His ego was heavily stroked and unfortunately gold-diggers and fair-weather friends remained invisible to Ash.

Basking in this new glory, he drifted away from Suraya and the days of abundance. He believed that his new abundance was better, and no matter how long he left the tap running, it never ran dry. There was plenty of laughter, back-slapping, and unsavoury jokes about the less fortunate. Credit was also easy to come by. Ash was a big spender living in the now, too busy looking out of the front windscreen to bother checking his rear-view mirror. His sharks were closer than he suspected.

Arrogance is never appealing. One should respect and appreciate the gifts life bestows on one, and thumbing one's nose at the provider is bound to get noticed. In Ash's case, it did, and destiny was not at all impressed. She wanted Ash to be a role model and consequently was forced to intervene. Ash received his first warning. While overexerting himself at the gym, he tore a hamstring.

The injury was not career-threatening, but it was a clear warning. Ash was sidelined for an extended period, during which he was able to step back from his life and reflect. It was a sobering moment. He now realised that his new abundance was limited and had a sell-by date. While at the top of his game, he had not saved his money and, despite the abundance, his bank balance reflected a large overdraft. He also noticed that the pack of back-slapping friends and gorgeous women had thinned. Circumstances now revealed that it was Ash who might have been the fool.

The enforced layoff also allowed Ash to focus on his financial situation. The news was not good; he owed a lot of money. He hoped that when he recovered, he could regain his place in the national team, pay off his debts, and set himself up with a secure nest egg. He dreamt of a large house, flashy cars, and a beautiful wife. Like all his other sports-star buddies, he hoped to start a family. When he visited his church, he knelt down, bowed his head in prayer, and begged to be given a second chance.

For a while, it seemed Ash's plea had been heard. There were the odd delays, but the injury was healing well. He rejoined the national squad and was looking forward to resuming his place in the team. But the parties and women did not cease, as he had so clearly agreed to in his covenant. Destiny noticed this omission. She smiles in the face of the ungrateful. She required her role model to be humble and decided to dip him again.

One morning, while warming up in the gym, Ash's hamstring tore for a second time. He found himself prostrate on the training mat with an excruciating pain shooting up his leg. In a blinding flash of white light, the pain took over; time stood still. Ash felt he was drifting outside of himself, and it was in this space that destiny delivered her emphatic message.

5

Ash knew immediately that his sporting career was over. This put a swift and final end to the big paydays, the chanting crowds, the laughter, the women, and the back-slapping. All were swept away in one clean swoop. What had been, had been; the party was over, the tap ran dry. He was bankrupt and destitute. His reality check had arrived.

As his teammates filed out of the training facility, Ash knew that it was goodbye to the squad, forever. He was left to face his demons alone. The blood drained from his head; he felt nauseous. Ash felt as if he were slowly falling backwards into a deep dark hole, the bottom of which he could not see. Falling, falling, falling.

Ulysses no more.

CHAPTER 2
FLIGHT

F orced to flee the City of Gold, Ash returned to the only place he understood—home. Getting there involved flying, and he feared flying.

In order to be as unobtrusive as possible, he arrived at OR Tambo airport early, checked in his baggage, and secured a window seat. He hoped this and a few "calming pills" would ease his phobia. After receiving his boarding pass, he sought out a quiet corner in a restaurant where he could hide behind a newspaper and a cup of coffee. Choosing a table where he could sit with his back to the public, he lost himself in the daily paper.

While taking an order at the next table, the waitress dropped her pen. It bounced across the floor and landed under Ash's table. Being a gentleman, he bent down to retrieve it but couldn't reach it, so he got down on his hands and knees and crawled under the table. The waitress blushed when Ash emerged from under the table and handed her the pen.

"Thank you." She smiled and gave a delicate curtsy.

The customer whom she was serving had a ringside seat and appreciated Ash's chivalry. When he caught Ash's eye, he raised his finger to his brow and smiled. Ash gave a brief nod of acknowledgement and then returned to his hiding place. Next he swallowed his calming pills with some coffee.

By the time his flight was called, the pills had taken effect nicely. He was relaxed and felt as if he were floating. He joined the queue, boarded the plane, and took his seat. Staring out the window, he studied the sky. A dark storm was approaching. This unnerved him.

As the passengers were boarding, Ash kept an eye open to see who would be seated next to him; much to his relief, nobody came. But just as the cabin door was about to close, one last passenger arrived.

The new person was a small, clean-shaven man who weaved his way quickly up the aisle, heading straight for the empty seat next to Ash. Examining his boarding pass, he checked the seat number, then looked at Ash and confirmed that this was his seat. He sat down, and once comfortable, addressed Ash.

"Hey, that was such a kind thing you did!"

Ash needed reminding; he couldn't recall doing something cool.

"The waitress with the pen. She was serving me."

Oh, great, thought Ash. *A sports fan. They* tended to know Ash better than he knew himself, and they were well aware of his plummet to disgrace.

"TK," said the sports fan, extending his hand.

Ash acknowledged the greeting with an awkward "Huh," and then continued looking out the window, his escape route.

As the plane taxied out to the runway, a firm female voice came over the intercom. "Since we will be flying close to a thunderstorm, the captain requests that you kindly remain seated and keep your seatbelts fastened throughout the flight. We will be landing in Cape Town in two hours, where we expect good weather and a pleasant evening."

Ash took this as a warning and didn't hear the pleasantries that followed. His chest had already started to tighten, and he feared the worst. He stared out of the window in the hope of calming his fear, but the storm was much closer.

The plane came to a halt at the end of the runway as the pilot revved the engines. As the plane shuddered and strained at its leash, the tightness in Ash's chest grew. When the pilot unleashed the plane and it sprang forward, Ash felt his heart rate quicken. He looked out of the window; the grass on the edge of the runway moved past, faster and faster. Little beads of sweat appeared on his forehead. The white lines on the runway began to blur. His claustrophobia was closing in. Ash felt the nose of the plane rise and was sucked into the back of his seat as the plane took off. He gripped the armrest so tightly that the skin on his knuckles bleached white.

Lightning flashed against the dark storm. Strong winds were beginning to buffet the plane. There was a loud thud from the undercarriage. The plane groaned and shuddered as it hit turbulence. Ash couldn't breathe, and his claustrophobia changed to panic. A pungent odour of sweat burst from his armpits. Then the plane hit an air pocket and fell. Ash got his fingers under his tie and ripped it away. Just as panic took hold, Ash saw a blinding flash of light and his world went silent. Once again, Ash found himself floating outside of his body.

"Relax, mate, relax. Breathe," called a gentle voice.

The plane hit the bottom of the air pocket with a crash.

"Steady, mate, steady. Don't stress. Breathe," called the voice, slowing him down. Ash felt a warm hand on his.

"Relax," the voice called again. "Take it easy."

Slowly the claustrophobia eased its grip. His mind began to focus, and he found that he could breathe. If he could just stretch his toes and touch the earth, he would feel much better.

The plane was now climbing easily.

Ash's lights flickered back on, and thought returned to him. He looked about, as if he were waking from a dream and was surprised to find himself on a plane. It was as if he had been away to a very quiet place with a bright white light. Ash became aware of the gentle hum of the engines and hushed conversations. He looked around. TK wore a worried look. The air hostess, who had been watching with alarm, hurried over with two bottles of water.

"Thank you," she said to TK, handing them both a bottle.

"No problem," said TK, but their eyes told a different story.

Ash took a sip of water and shook his head, his composure returning.

"You don't like flying?"

"No." Ash shook his head. "Not at all. Take-off and landings terrify me."

"And flying?"

"I can deal with that."

TK breathed a sigh of relief and sat back in his seat. *Whew!*

"Thanks," said Ash, mopping his brow as his pulse slowed. "Please excuse me. I try my best to control my fear, but the thunderstorm and air pockets freak me out."

"If I thought about it, I would probably react the same way. But I don't think about it," responded TK.

"Ash," said Ash, extending his hand. TK took it.

Eager to steer Ash away from his fear of flying, TK, being well aware of Ash's rugby career, broached the subject of sport. "What are you going to do now that you have retired?"

"I'm not sure," said Ash. "I need to start again."

"What do you mean?"

"Should I say I am between careers?"

"No," said TK, shaking his head in disbelief.

"I have been a fool."

"Not that it's any of my business, but why do you say that?"

"You're right," said Ash, "it's none of your business." With that barbed comment, he switched TK off again.

Ash turned his face to the window. He had a vivid recollection of the white light and remained stunned by the power of the experience. He recalled a similar jolt in the gym and began to reflect. This seemed to be a coincidence; either something was wrong or possibly it was a message from the great beyond. Like the plane passing through air, he was passing through life. He had made mistakes, he had been humiliated, he was broke, and his self-image shattered, but he was still alive. He who had flown so high was now humbled and feeding on the ground with the pigeons. This humbling was a difficult pie to eat and Ash doubted he had the strength to endure the shame. Ending his life seemed to be a reasonable deliverance. He reviewed his options. Finally, he settled on one that seemed to be the most plausible: drowning. He could make that look like an accident.

Unknown to Ash, destiny had never left his side and was presiding over events. It was she who had brought him to this crossroads, and now that life had tenderised Ash sufficiently, it was time for him to begin the next chapter in his life. For this he needed a new guide: the Goddess of Good Luck. She was perfect for the job. She had the right qualifications and a sense of humour, and her exacting examinations often came in the form of practical jokes. Her students needed to recognise temptation, and she tested them frequently, often finding their reactions amusing.

Ash did not realise his potential. She did. Having survived the first part of his education, he was still in good physical shape, and though he didn't know this yet, he was about to be transformed into a role model. Having been dipped in experience, he now needed to cure. The Goddess would see to this. But arrogance and indulgence were qualities she abhorred, and she took steps to iron these crinkles out of her students. These lessons were often painful but seemed to be the only medicine that worked on stubborn students.

After being jolted by the white light, Ash's mind was now clear and primed. The Goddess seized the moment and set to work on her new student. It was she who brought the drinks trolley with the coffee that broke the ice between Ash and TK, and it was she who gave TK the words he sought.

"Everybody has to drop the ball. That's how we learn."

"True," said Ash, reflecting on the wisdom.

"You were doing so well. Bummer about the hammy. I hope you have avoided the fate of so many sports stars," replied TK.

"What fate is that?" asked Ash wearily.

"When their careers end abruptly, they find they are broke."

Looking down at the earth floating far below, the words popped out of his mouth before his brain had time to cut them. "That's me."

"What do you mean?" asked TK, astonished.

"I'm broke."

The Goddess noticed the surrender.

"I don't get it," said TK.

Once again, Ash found himself despondently looking down at the world floating miles below. "During my recent recovery," he admitted, "I worked out what a fool I have been. When I got my break, I was too young and too inexperienced to know what to do with all the money." There was an exhausted sadness in his voice. "I didn't know how to cope with the fame and was too afraid to ask. I spent my good fortune as if the tap would never run dry. It did, and I was caught off sides."

The Goddess noticed Ash's surrender turn to submission and was pleased.

"But not dumb," said TK, trying to cheer him up.

"Thank you," said Ash. "That's kind of you, but I was stupid."

"What happened?" asked TK.

"While I was recovering, I began to see that many of the people around me were 'pretend' friends. All they'd really wanted was my cash. When I needed them, they disappeared, and by the time I woke up, I was deeply in debt with nothing to show. I'd hoped to recover, get back into the team, settle my debts, and build a nest egg. But then I got injured again, and that put an end to that dream."

"What have you got to show for your good fortune?" asked TK.

"A pile of debts and some memories," grunted Ash in an offhand manner.

"Will you ever play rugby again?"

"No. The doctors advise against it."

"You never married?"

"No. I dropped the person who loved me the most."

Ash thought this TK man was becoming annoying, yet despite his best efforts to shut his mouth, his honest words just kept tumbling out.

"A big mistake?"

"Yeah," said Ash. "I would give anything to have her back." He sounded sorry.

"Anything?"

"Yep."

"So what now?" asked TK, slowly baiting the hook?

"I will have to start again, but I don't know where."

"Don't be too hard on yourself," said TK. "There is some good news."

"What's that?"

"You have learnt how to recognise a 'gift horse.'"

"… and lose one," admitted Ash. A small smile of acknowledgement tickled the corners of his mouth. He sure knew how to lose gift horses.

"You seem to have learnt from your mistakes."

"Yeah." Ash nodded. "An expensive lesson."

"Failure is part of the journey. It contributes to success," said TK.

"I tried to fly too high. My wings melted." Ash had a good point. His behaviour had been found wanting. Regrets? He had a few; some of which he would have preferred to forget.

"We all need humbling."

"True."

The Goddess did a double take. Ash was making excellent progress.

"All is definitely not lost," said TK.

"What do you mean?" Ash half-snapped at TK. *Couldn't the man see?* He, Ash, was stuffed. Finished. Kaput. Only two choices lay ahead: humble pie or a big swim.

"You've only lost your cash, that's all," prodded TK. "Don't underestimate the value of that lesson. We can only become truly wealthy when we have learnt the value of what we have."

"True," conceded Ash.

"So now you arrive at this crossroads. It's a good time to ask, what do I want out of life?"

Ash looked at TK out of the corner of his eye; he didn't like trick questions because they usually made him look stupid, but he conceded that TK did have a point. He had some thinking to do.

"You have experience," continued TK, "but you are broke. In essence, you are now free to decide what you want from life. You didn't need a disaster to realise this truth. This 'popcorn moment' is always present," said TK, examining his nails in a casual manner, "but it usually takes a disaster to bring it into urgent focus. Unfortunately, you seem to have chosen the difficult path for yourself and adversity has now brought you to this moment."

Ash looked at TK intently. He did not like where this conversation was going, but there was little he could do because he was still being swept along by the spell of the white light.

"You can only make a plan if you know where you want to go," invited TK. "Do you have a destination in mind?"

TK sort of stuck the question under Ash's rib and then dug it in; a solid jab.

"No," said Ash.

"To answer that question," said TK adventurously, "you must define what you want from life and then develop a plan that will turn your vision into reality. Without a destination, there can be no journey."

Ash looked down at the world floating beneath the clouds. Maybe he would hold off on that big swim for a while. Humiliation was no easy pie to eat, but maybe it had substance, and TK had hinted at a possible silver lining.

"Want do you want most out of life?" prompted TK again, not allowing Ash to settle.

"I want to be wealthy," said Ash.

"What does wealth mean to you?"

"You are wealthy when you have a lot of money," said Ash, looking at TK as if he came from another planet.

"Only money?" queried TK.

"Without money you are stuffed."

"That problem can be solved," said TK. "There is a simple way to create a fountain of money."

Ash was intrigued; he liked the idea of having his own personal fountain of money. If he could have, he would have ordered a bunch of them yesterday.

"It's simple," said TK matter-of-factly. "Even if you are poor, you can become wealthy. Financial security is available to all, no matter how difficult your circumstances. Everybody can be financially free."

Yeah right, mused Ash as he began to allow himself to like TK a little bit. He acknowledged that maybe he had been wrong to switch TK off. He resolved to go with the conversation and let it guide him, like the wind in the wheat fields.

Ash examined TK more closely. TK had a gentle face and a youthful smile and his hair was all over the place.

"Describe wealth," prodded TK.

"When you have a lot of money!" confirmed Ash.

"Is that all? Just money?" asked TK, examining his fingernails again. "What does it take for you to be content with life? Financial freedom is important, but it's not everything."

Ash looked pensive for a second or two. "No," disagreed Ash. "Without money you are really stuffed."

"Real wealth," persisted TK, "includes financial security, but it also includes love, a family, a home, friends, and a healthy environment. When you assess true wealth, you would also want to include lifestyle aspects, like being stress free, at peace with oneself and life."

"You have a point," acknowledged Ash, warming to the conversation. "But at the moment that seems a very long way away."

"Not really," said TK, dangling the hook a little closer.

"I can only think about money right now," said Ash. He couldn't see it any other way.

"That's the thing—people are taught how to work for money, not how money can work for them," replied TK.

This comment sparked Ash's attention. He hadn't heard money referred to like that before.

"You just have to look at the equation the other way around," continued TK. "It's easy to create a Money Fountain; all you need to be is consistent and patient and you will be financially free."

Rubbish! thought Ash.

But TK wouldn't let it go. "Financial security is available to all."

Ridiculous! Ash looked out of the window.

"If you follow the rules, maybe you can even win back your lost love," said TK, invoking Suraya, and with her came Mr February's abundance. Ash began to recognise the enormity of his loss.

"Yeah, sure," said Ash sarcastically.

At that moment, Ash was too confused to realise that he was in the presence of the Goddess of Good Luck, but years later, when he looked back over the invisible path his life had followed, he would realise that this was one of those moments that had changed his life for the better.

"There is a practical, easy-to-implement way to create great wealth," said TK.

Ash adjusted his seat to the upright position.

"What's that?"

"The secret of the Money Fountain."

Ash started paying closer attention.

"There are three secrets to the Money Fountain," said TK. "Each secret has an operating system. Once you get the operating systems in place, the fountain starts flowing."

Ash saw an image of a fountain of dollars.

"And the longer you stick to the rules, the faster your fountain will flow," said TK.

Ash saw a mighty deluge of wealth flowing towards him from his Money Fountain.

"Eventually, you will struggle to give the money away," added TK.

Ash saw himself giving away bundles and bundles of cash.

"All you have to do is keep to the rules," said TK.

Ash wanted to know more.

"It's not easy bringing everything into line," granted TK. "But when you do, it works 100 percent. Follow the rules, and you will create a never-ending stream of wealth for yourself and your children. You will never be poor again, and your children will go to work for entertainment value only."

TK spoke with a deep confidence, which Ash noticed.

"Why don't people know about this?" challenged Ash.

"Financial institutions invest your money in their Money Fountain, and then give you the small change to keep you quiet."

Ash looked stunned.

"That is why they are rich, and you are not."

This took the wind right out of Ash's sails.

"When you apply the secrets of the Money Fountain to your own money," said TK jovially, "then all your money flows into your fountain as it always should have, not via somebody else's fountain. The reason they don't tell you how a Money Fountain works is because they are helping themselves to your share."

It was as if Ash had been slapped. This could not be true.

"How can I create a Money Fountain for myself?" asked Ash enthusiastically.

"Oh," said TK in an offhand manner. "The system is simple and it works."

"Could you teach me how to make one?" asked Ash, accepting the baited hook.

"Depends," said TK, becoming slippery. If Ash wanted to know more, he would have to show some commitment.

Thrilled as she was by the progress Ash was making, the Goddess required her students be tested. Having dipped her student into the pool of knowledge, she now needed to test him. How much fight did he have? Knowing Ash's fear of landing, she prodded the air hostess into action.

"Please stow your cabin baggage and fasten your seatbelts. We will be landing in ten minutes. Cape Town is a pleasant 17 C° degrees."

As she spoke, Ash saw his claustrophobia appear from behind the curtain and stare at him. He started to become uncomfortable and forgot about the Money Fountain. Then he saw his claustrophobia slithering down the aisle towards him. His chest began to constrict.

"Relax, Ash. Breathe. Be gentle," encouraged TK, patting his hand. "Stretch your toes down and see if you can touch the earth."

Ash tried and found that if he imagined it, he could stretch his toes all the way down and touch the earth; and when they touched the earth, he found he could breathe and his hands relaxed their grip on the armrests. He took a sip of water and looked out of the window. Snow-capped mountains drifted below; puffy clouds glowed orange in the sunset. Cold mists hugged the valleys. Soon the city lights became visible in the distance. As the plane came in to land, the lights turned into strings of fairy lights set against the silhouette of Table Mountain, etched on a sky of gold. Ash was coming home broken and broke. *Is this what experience does to young adults?* he wondered. *Forces them to grow up? And what does growing up mean?*

It means taking responsibility, said a voice deep inside his head.

The nose of the plane rose, the flaps engaged, and the engines roared. The wheels touched the ground with a thud and the plane bounced. The nose of the plane came down and the front wheels touched the earth. The plane slowed. Ash was safe. He relaxed. The flight had panned out to be more than he had expected. He'd seen a white light, a glimmer of a silver lining, and a Money Fountain. Was this a gift horse? Was this a new path opening before him?

"It was nice meeting you, Ash," said TK, unbuckling his seatbelt.

"Same," said Ash, but as TK started to get up, Ash interrupted him. "Would you be prepared to teach me about the Money Fountain?"

"Maybe," said TK, smiling.

"No. I'm serious," said Ash. "I have been humbled. I believe I have learnt my lesson."

"Maybe you have," said TK. "Here's my card. Call me. The ball's in your court."

CHAPTER 3
THE GARDENS

The day Ash caught the bus into Cape Town he had a special step in his gait. TK had agreed to teach him how to create a Money Fountain, and he was on his way to meet him in the Company Gardens in the heart of the city.

He alighted at the City Hall because the narrow streets and old buildings reminded him of Europe. He walked up past the Slave Lodge, which housed a collection of dark history—his history. Ash still had no idea that he himself might be enslaved; this realisation lay in the future.

Then he turned into Government Avenue and walked past the Houses of Parliament, which had recently been painted a dark maroon with white trim and now looked like a gingerbread house. As he entered the Company Gardens, time slowed and nature asserted itself; the hubbub of the city quietened. Squirrels begged, but Ash declined their eloquent appeals. He enjoyed feeding them, but he had a date with TK and hurried along; anticipation and the hope of release had embraced him.

Set below the thousand-metre cliffs of Table Mountain, this garden was a refuge from the money madness that gripped the city. Its tranquillity was filled with the sound of bird calls and tinkling fountains. Well-manicured lawns hugged bright flower beds and large trees shaded dark groves. The coral trees were in full bloom, as was the magnolia. Ash walked slowly through the dripping vines of the Japanese pagoda and emerged at the entrance to the outdoor eatery. TK, who was early, was just finishing a cup of coffee. When he saw Ash, he smiled and waved.

"Would you like a coffee?" asked TK as Ash seated himself.

"Yes, please."

While TK was negotiating the order with the waitress, Ash looked around. The outdoor dining area was dominated by a large gum tree and furnished with downmarket green plastic garden furniture. A few pigeons patrolled the paving looking for morsels that had fallen from the plates of the affluent. Ash empathised.

When the cappuccinos arrived, Ash noticed that the foam was full of bubbles and almost transparent. When he poured a sachet of sugar onto his foam, it sank straight through and disappeared.

"That happens when the milk is too hot," said TK, pointing to the bubbles in the foam. "In order to make perfect foam, the milk mustn't get hotter than 63°C. When you make foam for a cappuccino, you are only meant to skim the top of the milk with the steam. That's the screaming noise one hears," observed TK. "But the person who made this cup inserted the nozzle into the milk and boiled it. That's why there are bubbles in the foam. Good foam should have fine bubbles and appear solid. It should also be able to support the weight of a sachet of sugar. To be honest, the coffee is not good, but it is a small detail. I come here for the fresh air, the birds, and the mountain. And you are all important to me today."

Ash was honoured and thanked TK and then steered the conversation back to his quest.

"The Money Fountain," said Ash. "I am keen to know more."

"Ah, yes, the Money Fountain," said TK. "How to create a stream of money that flows endlessly towards you in such a manner that the flow grows bigger and faster with each passing day?"

"That's the one," said Ash.

"Wealth flows like a river," said TK. "In order to attract it, you need to meet certain basic criteria. Wealth seldom arrives in one hit; it comes from hard work, diligence, consistent saving, and considered investments. This does not mean that if you have a small salary you are denied the right to be wealthy. Neither does it mean that to be wealthy you need to be stingy or live in extreme denial. Creating a Money Fountain is a measured approach over time, and after twenty-five years, you will be financially independent."

"Free?" asked Ash.

"Yes," said TK, repeating the period of twenty-five years.

"Twenty-five years? That sounds doable."

"If you like, I will mentor you."

"How much will it cost?"

"Nothing. But whatever I teach you, you are obliged to pay it forward."

"What's that?"

"Whatever you receive for free, you will in turn give for free. Is that fair?"

"It's fair," said Ash.

"Your word is taken as final," said TK.

"Accepted," said Ash. The two men shook hands.

TK started by introducing the Goddess of Good Luck. "She is a positive spirit that is available to all of us. It is she who selects and introduces new students. When she does, something out of the ordinary happens."

Ash didn't understand.

"Something that shouldn't happen does happen. That is how we recognise new members."

Ash still didn't get it.

"Remember when you were at OR Tambo airport and the waitress's pen slipped under your table?"

"Yes." Ash did remember.

"You didn't know it then, but that was your introduction. When I sat down next to you on the plane, I knew who you were."

"I was rude," said Ash apologetically.

"All new students are," said TK patiently. "That's because they are trying to hide their humiliation."

Ash nodded. He remembered this as well.

"The Goddess has chosen to introduce you to the Fellowship."

"The Fellowship?" asked Ash.

"Yes. There are quite a few of us, and we were all introduced in a similar fashion. Some become mentors like me, and others, who are specialists in their field, become tutors. Once you have been taught, and you begin to reap the benefits, you will become a mentor, bound by the pay-it-forward principle. What we receive for free we are honour-bound to share."

Ash nodded. He understood.

"The Fellowship is committed to bringing financial liberation to the world. Our ultimate destination is conscious wealth."

"What does that mean?" asked Ash curiously.

"Conscious wealth is a process whereby we create wealth that is beneficial to the environment."

"Isn't wealth based on exploitation?"

"It does not have to be," said TK emphatically. "Like a natural spring, the Money Fountain brings life and peace."

Ash was intrigued. A butterfly hovered near the table.

"Part of your mentorship is about encouraging good luck to your side," continued TK. "We refer to good luck as 'the Goddess' or 'the Goddess of Good Luck.' She favours the brave, but she is delicate, like a butterfly," said TK, pointing to a black-and-yellow butterfly flitting past their table. "And just like a butterfly, wealth finds it hard to settle. You will come to realise that both need to be treated with respect."

Ash began to reflect on the folly of his indulgences.

"Establishing this relationship takes time and perseverance. Through your thoughts and actions, you create your own luck."

"Like when you look after the pennies the pounds take care of themselves," said Ash.

"Exactly," said TK, and then he continued. "Even though the Goddess has chosen you, she will wait for you to reveal your intentions before she decides to back you. This relationship is up to you. If you deviate from the path, she will leave you. This is the same with wealth. There are certain basic rules that you need to stick to."

"I find myself at a crossroads," said Ash. "And I can only create my future once I have defined my destination."

"Excellent," laughed TK. "You are a fast learner. Great wealth is not a matter of chance; it is about practice and repetition and making your own luck. The more you practise, the luckier you become."

"Like golf?"

"Correct!" said TK, complimenting Ash. "After you have practised a swing five hundred times, it becomes natural. Repetition is the key."

Ash nodded.

"But be warned," said TK. "The Goddess does not like gambling, so whatever you do, keep away from get-rich-quick thoughts. Do not buy a lottery ticket."

"Why not?" asked Ash.

"Because dreams of big wins usually bear little more than fantasies. Wealth creation is a simple, structured plan that requires diligence and repetition."

An explosive boom reverberated across the city, causing the pigeons to fly up in alarm. The butterfly darted away.

"Ah, the noonday gun," said TK, without missing a beat. "In the process of wealth creation, the aim is to conduct yourself in such a manner that the

Goddess is attracted to you. When she does arrive, she will open doors for you. She wants you to succeed."

Presently, the pigeons returned to their ground patrol and the butterfly danced nervously among the flowers. Peace slowly returned to the garden. Ash could hear the fountain tinkling again. It settled him.

"The Goddess enjoys the company and protection of honest, diligent people who work hard, save their money, and invest well. She favours the brave and creates opportunities for them. So never procrastinate when a gift horse is visiting in your paddock. Strike when opportunity presents itself."

The butterfly flitted back to the table and settled on the edge. Ash examined her black-and-yellow wings and extended a finger towards her. She apprehensively inspected his peace offering but remained unconvinced and flew away.

Ash smiled and nodded.

"There are certain things the Goddess does not like. She is repulsed by airs and graces, arrogance, gambling, and waste."

Ash swallowed hard. He understood the consequence of arrogance; it had led to his fall from grace.

"Honesty is the first step," said TK. "You might be able to delude yourself, but the Goddess will see straight through you, and only when you start being truthful with yourself can the Goddess begin to help you."

"Yeah, okay," admitted Ash. "I dropped the ball. Several balls."

TK took a close look at Ash's face and nodded.

"As your mentor, my job is to guide you, answer your questions, and, when necessary, arrange for you to meet your tutors: Dr Swan, Big Julius, and Mrs

Blumkin. Each is a specialist in a field of wealth creation. If you need more information, I will refer you to other specialists."

Ash stretched his arms above his head and felt his spine crack as the bones realigned themselves. He was alert and focussed. He took another sip of his cold coffee and repeated the three names. It sounded as if they came from a fairy tale.

"Shall we eat?" asked TK.

Ash was starving but disguised his hunger with a casual nod. After scanning the menu and as if speaking to himself, TK said, "The food's not great here. Best to stick to something simple like a cheeseburger. It's hard to screw that up."

"I'll go for the same."

TK waved to the waitress, who was chatting on her mobile. She ended the call and walked over to the table, smiling.

"Two cheeseburgers and two large Cokes," said TK.

After she'd left, TK addressed Ash. "Sorry about just ordering a Coke for you, mate. It's insurance against dodgy food."

Ash found himself smiling at this insight.

"The key to creating a Money Fountain is to pay yourself first. You do this by saving 10 percent of your income and investing it in a facility that compounds at a reasonable rate over time. As your intentions and actions become clear, the Goddess will take more notice of you. Until then, she will let you drift."

10 percent. Ash was surprised.

"She won't come immediately, but by starting to save, you will signal your intention, and she will start taking notice of you."

"What is a facility that compounds at a reasonable rate over time?" asked Ash.

"Let's not race ahead, shall we," said TK. "That is the job for your tutors. They are the specialists and will reveal this knowledge to you in the correct sequence."

Swan, Big Julius, and Blumkin. Ash wondered who these other people were.

The butterfly returned and alighted on the table. Ash felt as if she was gazing at him, and he marvelled at her beauty. "Hello, butterfly," he said softly.

"You understand that wealth is not just about money," TK responded. "Enjoy your life, fall in love, laugh, and look after your health. These are also important aspects of wealth. Look after your body because without it you have nothing. It is the temple of your soul. There's a story that goes with this," TK continued.

One day a genie appears before a young man and says to him, "Young man, you can have any car you want. Name your choice."

The young man is naturally taken by surprise and reflects on the offer. Being cautious, he smells a rat. So he says to the genie, "Thank you. This is a very generous offer, but it seems too generous. There must be a catch."

Embarrassed at having been caught out so quickly, the genie sheepishly admits that there is indeed a catch. "You can only ever have this one car. It has to last your whole life."

"What do you mean?" asked the young man.

"Just that," said the genie. "You get to choose any car you like, but it has to last a lifetime."

After thinking about the proposition for a while, the young man realised that as he planned to live for a long time, he would have to look after that car carefully. He would have to garage it, service it regularly, wash it, and if it was in an accident, repair it. A flashy sports car would be expensive to maintain. That wouldn't work.

"So the windfall is more about looking after the gift?" said Ash.

"Exactly," said TK. "And the gift the genie is referring to is your body. You only get one, and it has to last a lifetime. This is one of the key principles of creating a Money Fountain; look after your health and emotional well-being. Money is just a part of the plate. Family, friends, living a life of significance, inner wealth, spirituality, and caring about the environment are all important aspects of true wealth, and you need to pay them all equal attention. Grow plants and marvel at evolution because they are God's greatest creation."

The waitress arrived with lunch and placed the two cheeseburgers and two glasses of Coke on the table. The butterfly flew away.

"Perfect. Thank you," said TK.

TK salted his chips and squirted a reservoir of tomato sauce onto his plate. Then he lifted the lid of his burger and filled that with tomato sauce, mayonnaise, and mustard and then squashed it down on the patty. Sauce oozed from the sides. Ash sensed that for the next few minutes TK would be revealing the secrets to wealth around chips, through a cheeseburger, and over iced Coca-Cola. But he didn't mind. Ash sought knowledge and so he was prepared to tolerate TK's burger indulgence. Besides, the more TK spoke, the more time he had to enjoy his meal, and he was hungry.

"Focus on the good things in life. Forgive and do not bear grudges," said TK, now talking through his burger. "They hold you back. Choose carefully which worries you care to be involved in. Don't get upset by politicians; if you don't like one party, simply give your energy to another. Getting upset about something is merely an excuse to not focus on what is important, and that is growing your Money Fountain."

Ash nodded.

"There are three secrets to creating a Money Fountain. They form a triangle. Each side of the triangle has operating principles that define the strategy and attitude." TK shaped his thumbs and forefingers in a triangle.

"When you apply the operating system of each side of the triangle and they begin to work together, then you will create your own never-ending fountain of wealth," continued TK. "It is fail-safe. The only thing that can prevent you from achieving your goal is if a meteorite collides with the earth and wipes us out."

This guarantee impressed Ash.

"Stick to the rules and you will be financially secure."

"I find that hard to believe," said Ash, eating his chips first.

"It's a grand statement," said TK with confidence. "But it is true."

"That's incredible," said Ash.

TK smiled. The baited hook had a nibbler.

"Wealth is attracted to those who save. This is the most important point. Fail here and you may as well put on the handcuffs and throw away the key. If you fail, you will remain enslaved."

"Enslaved?" Ash frowned. "What do you mean?"

"Unless you start saving 10 percent of your take-home pay, you will always be poor. This is the first secret to wealth. Once you do this, then you can start investing in something that offers you the compounding effect. That is the 'Magic Penny.'"

"What is that?" asked Ash.

"The Magic Penny is the eighth wonder of the world," laughed TK. "Like magic, money correctly invested multiplies endlessly, and the longer you stick with the plan, the faster it grows. Saving 10 percent of your take-home pay is the source of the Money Fountain, which creates a never-ending stream of cash that flows towards you."

Ash found this hard to believe.

"The next operating principle has to do with protection," said TK, dipping a chip. "In order for the Goddess to feel more comfortable around you, she needs security and protection. This means you must take out life insurance and make a will."

"A what?" asked Ash?

"Okay. We have quite a bit to do," said TK, crunching on a crispy chip. "A will is a legal document that determines what happens to your estate when you die."

Then he looked at Ash with concern. "Do you know what an estate is?"

"No," said Ash.

"Right," said TK, looking into the distance. "That's your homework. Go and find out about life insurance and wills. When we next meet, I want to see proof of your having begun the process."

TK took up his knife and fork and focussed on his cheeseburger and licked his lips.

"The first thing to do is to get a job and create an income for yourself. Hard work attracts the good things in life. It works like this," said TK, cutting into his burger. "Once you get a job, apply yourself. Next, make work your friend. Enjoy your work and the people you work with. Have a light, happy approach to work, and appreciate the opportunities it brings. Study so that you can improve your skills and knowledge."

Ash was confused. In his mind, work was a necessary evil that disempowered people. Work was like selling your soul to the devil.

TK noticed and thought for a while. "Here's another story for you."

Jonas was a farm labourer. He wasn't paid well, but he was grateful for the opportunity and enjoyed the fresh air and company. As he and his fellow labourers were walking to work one day, he pointed to the neighbouring farmer's fields and said the labourers were not ploughing the fields deeply enough. The point he was trying to make was that the seedlings would find it hard to grow in the shallow trenches, but his workmates thought he was crazy and laughed at him. They said that those labourers were wise because who wanted to work hard for little pay?

A discussion began and Jonas tried to justify his position by pointing out that because those labourers were cutting corners they would reap a poor harvest, and this would put their jobs at risk. But the others only laughed louder. In the end, they agreed to disagree, and Jonas got marked as a potential traitor.

That didn't stop Jonas. He got great satisfaction from watching crops grow and was happy when he saw the fruits of their labour bloom into tall and healthy crops. He told his workmates that hard work and diligence brought good things in life. They laughed more and sniggered at Jonas. "Only a fool works hard for such little pay."

Jonas ignored them and persisted with his quest, making his fellow labourers plough the fields deeper. The farmer noticed Jonas arguing with the men but kept quiet. The seedlings grew easily in the well-ploughed field, and when the crop was harvested, the farmer noticed that it fetched a higher price than his neighbour's. Still, the farmer said nothing.

Jonas was not deterred by this omission and worked harder. In his spare time, he learnt all there was to learn about the crops they were planting and the best way to protect the crops from disease and insects. Then he applied his knowledge. The farmer noticed this as well.

When the next harvest was reaped, it again fetched a higher price. This time the farmer gave Jonas a raise and more responsibility. Jonas was also made a manager. In this way, he avoided being a labourer, but still he enjoyed working and worked harder. The farmer was impressed, so he gave Jonas a percentage of the harvest. This is how hard work and study attract wealth. The other labourers got left behind.

Ash took another sip of his Coke. It was cold and helped the burger settle.

"That doesn't sound flash," said Ash, "and I guess it won't attract gold-diggers."

"What's the moral of the story?" prodded TK, encouraging his student forwards.

Ash was unsure.

"Enjoy your work; even if it's hard, it is vital to wealth creation. First step, create a financial stream that you can grow, then apply yourself."

Ash nodded. He could do this.

"When you work hard, you make yourself attractive to employers, and in this way hard work attracts money and good things."

"But how hard should one work?"

"Hard work does not mean you have to sell your soul," said TK. "The pursuit of wealth leaves much room for spiritual growth; work so that you can live, don't live so that you can work. That's slavery. Financial wealth is not your primary focus. It is a by-product of a contented, focussed lifestyle."

Ash nodded.

"How much you have to work is directly linked to your expenses."

Ash didn't understand.

"If your debt is large, you will have to work harder and take bigger risks."

Ash chuckled at this insight.

"So enjoy your work and save 10 percent. That is the key to paying yourself first; never forget that."

"But how do I save 10 percent?" asked Ash.

"Dr Swan will explain that."

TK had managed to talk the whole way through his cheeseburger and now mopped up the remaining sauce with a few specially saved chips. When he'd finished the last chip, he beckoned to the waitress. "Thanks, love, that was delicious. Is your espresso any good?"

"Top drawer."

"Espresso, Ash?"

"Please."

"Two espressos, please, ma'am."

"Coming up."

"Look, Ash," said TK. "I have to fly in a few minutes, but you've got my card. Call me when you're ready, and I'll set up the meetings with your tutors. They will explain the secrets and their operating systems to you."

Ash was a little downcast. He wanted all the information in one quick fix, and TK's referrals suggested time and effort, which he was not that keen to commit to. The Goddess noticed this.

"You are too kind," said Ash.

"Humbled," said TK. "We all have the Goddess to thank."

"I am beginning to understand."

"Do you have a car?" asked TK.

"Yes," said Ash, lying. He had lost everything in the implosion, including his flashy car.

"Good, because Big Julius lives a little way away and you will need to drive."

At this moment, their espressos arrived and TK requested the bill.

"Before you go, please tell me, why are you taking so much trouble with me?" asked Ash.

"For some reason, the Goddess likes you. *She* chose you. Your journey began when that pen bounced under your table. The Goddess rescued me too, and I am honour-bound to share the knowledge I have received for free. Now it's my turn to mentor you. It will be the same for you."

While Ash had not yet come to believe in the forgiving hand of destiny, the Goddess was present and not entirely impressed with him. Quite correctly, she had noticed Ash's reticence to commit to the programme. He was still looking for easy solutions and did not yet appreciate the sting of desperation. It seemed another lesson was required.

Ash and TK finished their coffees and agreed to meet again when Ash called. They shook hands and optimistically parted company.

As Ash made his way back to the bus stop, the Goddess caused a pretty girl to stumble into him. Ash noticed her, but he did not notice the pickpocket. When he dug into his pocket at the bus stop, his wallet was gone. In it was TK's card. Once again, destiny welcomed Ash back to hardship.

His mettle would be tested.

CHAPTER 4
GREED

A cold drizzle had settled over the city the day Ash parked his rust bucket under the Norfolk pines and looked down on little Kalk Bay Harbour. Brightly painted wooden fishing boats were moored against the protecting harbour wall, at the far end of which was a quaint lighthouse—Ash's intended destination.

Cold, wet days were Ash's favourite because they kept most folks indoors, and this left the best places to him. Being quiet, such settings gave him time and space to be with his thoughts, and Ash needed to think. After losing his wallet, he had also lost TK, and since that day life had led him down a rocky road. He needed to reflect on this, and perhaps today was a good day for that last desperate swim.

Avoiding the puddles, he crossed the main road and climbed the stairs to the boardwalk. At the top he stopped and observed the arched railway bridge and the harbour waters lapping the beach. Some vagrants were packing up their night camp and preparing for a day's carousing. Funny, Ash thought to himself, how most people struggle to accumulate wealth, yet these people did not seem to care about money and were content without it. Money was not their god.

The train whistle drew his attention away from his contemplation. As he looked up, the train slipped out of the station and passed in front him. Ash followed it up the hill, crossed the tracks at the level crossing, and walked down the road to the harbour.

The mist hung low, catching the masts of the fishing boats. In the wheelhouse of one, a captain stood smoking and directing his crew. Lobster pods were piled high on the stern of most of the boats. Nets hung to rinse in the drizzle. The sea gurgled under the pier. A seal surfaced and lay on its back, staring at Ash. Then with a single flip of its tail, it glided under the water and disappeared. Mr February's abundance briefly visited Ash but left quickly.

Ash passed quietly behind the fishmongers and climbed the stairs to the harbour wall, the far side of which had been raised to form a bench. He climbed up onto the bench, peered over the wall, and looked down into the cold dark green sea. As the water rose and fell, it combed the long fronds of the kelp forest. Their dance reminded Ash of the wind gliding across the wheat fields. Again Mr February's abundance visited Ash but was soon driven off by his worries.

Ash pulled the hood of his jacket down over his head and strolled towards the end of the pier, where a fisherman sat dangling his line over the edge. He had a tackle box beside him, a bait bucket, and, optimistically, a catch bucket. If he did see Ash pass behind him, he did not acknowledge him.

Ash sat on the edge of the pier watching the waves pass just under his feet. If he needed to, it was just a little jump. He doubted the fisherman would hear his splash, and that would be the end of his shame.

Once he'd been a rich, famous rugby star who was now not able to escape his demons. Apart from losing his many opportunities, he had also managed to lose TK. Four years had passed since that day in the Company Gardens, and life had led him down a hard path and he now no longer knew which way to turn. Tired of the adversity, he felt like giving up. Reflecting back on things, he realised that he hadn't lost TK—it was destiny teaching him a new lesson. *Commitment.* He was convinced that the Goddess had noticed his desire to short-circuit the road to wealth and had sent him back to the school of hard knocks. But when he evaluated his life, he realised that the Goddess had not deserted him completely.

Having eaten his portion of humble pie, he'd begun to put his life back together. He had secured a job managing a hardware store. He did not know much about hardware, but he was popular and customers came to the store because of him. The turnover had climbed and shrinkage had fallen and his boss was pleased. Ash was also studying management. He had also returned to the mission station and sought out Suraya. This was the second time Ash had asked to be given a second chance. He was heard, and it went well. Suraya was suitably impressed with the new humble Ash and agreed to give him another chance. This was good because they both spoke the same language. Ash was now able to recognise a gift horse and showered her with appreciation. She gave him warmth, stability, and a home. They married in a small mission-station ceremony that lasted for the entire weekend. The stork of happiness also visited their home, and Ash counted their daughter as a further blessing. His job gave him stability; he was saving 10 percent of his income to buy a home. And this was how hard times found their way back into Ash's life.

In his urgency to create a Money Fountain, he discovered that money deposited in the bank grows very slowly, and in order to buy a house, he needed to grow his money faster. One day, his friend Selwyn offered him a chance to break the chains that bound him. Selwyn had put together a syndicate and was going to Thailand to buy emeralds. At first, Ash resisted, but Selwyn begged to be heard out and, being a gentleman, Ash relented. For a five-thousand-rand buy-in, Selwyn offered a guaranteed 300 percent return. Ash had asked for referees and had contacted them. They all spoke with confidence.

Ash did not tell Suraya when he withdrew their savings. Neither did he tell her about his bring-home-the-bacon-quick plan because he wanted it to be a surprise. In due course, his stones arrived, and, together, he and Suraya set out to consult an expert jeweller to have the stones valued.

While waiting to be attended to, they looked through the glittering glass-fronted cabinets of gold, diamonds, tanzanite, and rubies. Ash fell in love with the rose gold pendant and matching earrings with inset rubies. He saw these glowing on Suraya's chocolate skin. He wanted to buy this as a gift for her.

Ash handed his packet of stones to the jeweller, who placed them under a bright light and then affixed a magnifier to his eye and examined each stone scrupulously. After the jeweler had worked his way through the small pile, he took the magnifier from his eye and looked at the couple. The sadness and disappointment in his voice spoke louder than all the words. Ash felt himself falling slowly backwards into the dark cavern before he heard the words *fake, glass, sorry*.

Suraya had to dig deep into her well of forgiveness before she could begin work on her depressed husband, who eventually found the strength to pick himself up in his daughter's love and smile. He kept his job at the hardware store but did not tell his boss why Selwyn never came back to the store. Slowly life returned to normal and Ash continued saving 10 percent of his salary.

Once more, Ash found himself impatiently chafing at the restraint of the bank interest rate. He needed to make money quickly. One day, an associate from his rugby days approached him and offered him the chance to soar with the eagles again. Charles was an investment guru and offered him a 25 percent return per annum, plus the return of the initial investment in four years. Four years to double his money. This was the chance Ash was looking for. To buy in, a stake would cost R40 000. Ash did the math's and checked the references; they all sang off the same song sheet. The investment seemed sound. Without informing Suraya, he took the bait again.

Doubt started to visit Ash when he overheard some of the customers referring to Charles in loud voices, but as he had recently received his first two payments, he remained confident. He had called Charles to double-check, but Charles calmed his fears and promised to get back to him. The problem was that Ash wanted to believe Charles. On his way to work one morning, Ash bought the *Cape Times*, and to his great disappointment, saw Charles on the front page. Once more, Ash felt the earth crack open under his feet. Falling. Falling. The dark cavern had come to claim his life, again.

Perched on the edge of the breakwater, Ash tried to figure out what he was going to do about this new stuff-up. He now realised that without TK he was going nowhere. The drizzle mixed with his salty tears. How was he going to tell his wife?

When the Goddess stood back and observed Ash, she had to admit that her student did look thoroughly miserable; maybe it was time to give him another chance.

Ash watched the fisherman reel in a fish, unhook it, and drop it into the catch bucket. Then he re-baited the hook and cast it back into the water. Ash realised he had a lot in common with that little fish swimming round and round in the catch bucket. The stupid fish, he realised, swallows the bait whole and gets caught, while the cautious fish nibbles the bait from the hook and escapes with a full belly. Ash now understood that once again, he had been hooked by greed.

What were the secrets to the Money Fountain? TK had said money could work for you. But how? He had to find out. In his prayers, he pleaded for TK to be returned to him.

The drizzly Sunday morning found his prayers focussed on this longing. Ash understood that there was only one road forwards: tell Suraya, take it on the chin, and start again. He resolved to be more conservative with his savings and would no longer seek the shortcut to financial wealth. His days of soaring with the eagles were over. He was humbled and set off home to break the bad news to his wife.

It was still raining as he headed back to his car, and the hood of his jacket was still pulled tightly over his head.

"Ash?"

He didn't hear.

"Ash?" the voice shouted again.

Ash was lost in his thoughts and did not hear the feet running behind him.

The footsteps slowed next to him.

Still he did not hear.

A hand touched his forearm.

"Ash?"

Ash turned and looked into the man's face.

"TK?"

"Yes."

"TK?"

"Ash. What's wrong?"

"TK. Is it really you?" said Ash, grabbing both of TK's hands in his.

"None other."

Ash felt his knees buckle as he sank to the ground. Defeated. Subdued. Submitting. Exactly the way the Goddess wanted her student.

CHAPTER 5
DR SWAN

A sh had to climb a long, steep hill to reach Dr Swan's home. When he finally arrived, he needed a few minutes to compose himself before knocking on the heavy wooden door. After waiting a few minutes, he heard a key turning in the lock.

"Good morning, Dr Swan," said Ash as the door opened a crack. Cautious eyes peered at Ash from the shadow.

"And you are?" The voice sounded dignified but guarded.

"TK's friend Ash."

"What do you want?"

"TK said he had made an appointment for me."

"No. I don't recall that."

"Are you Dr Swan?"

"Yes."

"Well, then, there can't be a mistake," said Ash.

"No," said Dr Swan. "There is no mistake. I definitely don't have any appointments scheduled for today, but I do have a few moments to spare. Wait."

The door closed and Ash heard the sound of bolts and chains opening. Then the door opened and a tall, grey-haired gentleman emerged, warily studying Ash.

"Are you busy?" asked Ash optimistically.

"No."

"Well, then, could I speak with you?"

"Possibly."

"Would now be convenient?"

"Maybe," said Dr Swan, standing back and opening the door a little more. "Would you like to come in?"

"Yes, please."

Dr Swan swung open the heavy wooden door, motioned Ash through, and closed the door behind him with a solid shove. He tried the handle, making doubly sure the latch had caught, and then turned and ran his eyes up and down Ash, assessing him again.

Then, smiling, he took Ash by the arm and said, "Follow me, young man."

Dr Swan was built like a streamlined long-distance runner: tall, lean, with long, athletic legs and a light upper body. His bold Roman nose seemed designed to part the air as it passed over his handsome face. He formed his words as an English gentleman would, and his actions told of a cautious man. Ash placed him at a healthy sixty-five.

"Come through," said Dr Swan, ushering Ash into the lounge. "Would you like a nice cup of tea?"

"Thank you," said Ash.

"Make yourself comfortable while I brew the tea. If my daughter bothers you, please ignore her."

Before Ash could answer, Dr Swan disappeared, leaving him alone. He turned to take in the view. Wow! Set on the slopes of Table Mountain, Dr Swan's home looked east, across the Cape Flats to the distant Hottentots Holland Mountains, where the sun rose.

Dr Swan's home was refined, and the furnishings reflected a strong colonial influence. A bright painting of a dark-skinned man wearing a fez hung on one wall. It was an original Irma Stern, though Ash did not know this; he just liked the colours. The lounge and dining area faced a wall of glass; double doors led onto a polished patio, which opened up to sprawling lawns and a sparking pool. *Majestic,* thought Ash. The living area was decorated in shades of soft white and dark greens. A painting of Table Mountain hung in the lounge. Ash loved the light in this painting, though he did not know it was by South Africa's prominent landscape painter Thomas Baines. Soft background music filled the room with peace. Ash liked that as well but had no idea that it was *Cavatina*, a medley of classical Spanish guitar music pieces. Dr Swan's home exuded warmth and smelt of sandalwood with a hint of orange.

Just then, Dr Swan's daughter came down the stairs. Ms. Swan swaggered past Ash without acknowledging him. *Biff. Take that.*

Ash felt it.

Ms. Swan left a sweet-scented trail behind her. A delicate aroma in which Ash detected warm butter, a touch of rose, and then something pure, but he couldn't quite put his nose to it. Ash thought Dr Swan's daughter to be a bit like the view. Perfect.

Careful, little fish. You have been caught before. Ash heard the warning as he had heard the voice deep inside his mind before.

The young lady made her way across the patio, swishing her tail. It was at this point that Ash realised she was perfectly aware of his presence. A white butterfly fluttered across the lawn. Ash had grown up. He was wiser, and his experience at the University of Hard Knocks had taught him to recognise the hand of fate, and this time he was able to discern the Siren. The Goddess was checking to see how well her student was doing.

"I see you," said Ash, and then he smiled, and his smile grew into a chuckle—a warm hearty chuckle, like the one enjoyed with good friends. Ash felt comfortable.

"What's so funny?" asked Dr Swan, handing Ash a large mug of tea.

"Err, your home is fantastic, Dr Swan," stammered Ash.

"Please be seated," said Dr Swan, aware that Ash had sidestepped his question.

"Thank you." Ash struggled to fit onto the green leather couch and balance his mug on the armrest at the same time. Suddenly, he felt like a little boy, and that was fair because it's exactly what he looked like.

A new pilgrim, thought Dr Swan, *at the beginning of such an exciting journey.* When he was certain Ash was comfortable, he nailed him with a direct question.

"What were you laughing about?" Dr Swan was not smiling now.

Ash stared at the floor for a few moments, and then he looked up and met Dr Swan's gaze.

"I have been sidetracked by temptation too often. These mistakes have cost me dearly. When you came in, I was laughing because temptation and I now recognise each other."

"Remarkable," said Dr Swan, taking a sip of tea. "I spoke to TK while I was making the tea. He asked me to tell you about the first secret—pay yourself first. Why?"

"TK said if I humbled myself and learnt from my experience, you would teach me the first secret to the Money Fountain."

"Have you learnt these arts?"

"Which arts?"

"Being humble and recognising temptation?"

"Yes."

"Mm,…. Interesting," said Dr Swan, tapping his fingers on the armrest. "That's what TK said."

There was definitely something English about Dr Swan, and Ash liked it.

"Right," said Dr Swan. "Let's start at the beginning. I assume you're here because of your pursuit of wealth. So please tell me, what does wealth mean to you?"

"Before I met TK, in my old life, I thought wealth was about money and good times," said Ash boldly. "I have now come to understand that wealth is about health, love, family, environment, and contentment. Financial wealth offers security, but it is a means to an end. It is not everything. It's an important part of life, but it does not mean that one should sacrifice one's life in its pursuit. Wealth is about contentment and love."

"Ah," said Dr Swan, nodding. "You are correct. That is the essence of wealth. Our purpose is to create financial security, and we do that by creating a Money Fountain.

"This will not happen overnight," warned Dr Swan. "It will take twenty to twenty-five years, but after that, you and your children's children will be financially independent forever. In essence, they will be free. This is a promise. A Money Fountain will make this happen, but you will only succeed if you follow the rules. Are you with me?"

"I am," confirmed Ash.

"When I say 'follow the rules,'" said Dr Swan, "I don't mean follow them a little bit and cut some corners here and there; you need to follow the rules impeccably. Is that understood?"

Ash swallowed and nodded. Now he realised that the Fellowship was not a Mickey Mouse outfit.

"My purpose," said Dr Swan, "is to explain the operating system of the first and most important side of the triangle to you: pay yourself first. I will explain each point and how to implement it in sequence. If you don't implement each point in the correct sequence, your Money Fountain will not function. Understood?"

Ash nodded.

"There are no shortcuts," said Dr Swan. "If you commit to the programme, you will gain financial independence."

"I understand," said Ash, remembering his recent lessons on shortcuts and gift horses.

"If I understand TK correctly, you have a job and it sounds as if you are enjoying this. You have managed to save 10 percent of your income. You are married and have a child," said Dr Swan.

Ash nodded.

"You have done well. Don't underestimate the significance of your achievements. You are on the way to becoming financially independent."

"Thank you," said Ash, relaxing. "But I don't know who to trust with my 10 percent."

"I understand the pressing nature of your question," said Dr Swan. "But first things come first. Big Julius and Mrs Blumkin will explain how and what to do with your 10 percent. We are to discuss the pay-yourself-first principle, and there's quite a bit that goes into the finer details. My commitment to you is to explain these finer details."

"I am in your debt."

"We will see about that," chuckled Dr Swan, sitting further back on the couch. Then he cleared his throat with a small polite cough and focussed his mind.

"It is possible," he began, "to change R1 into R5 625 in twenty-five years. All you need is patience, time, and a bit of money. After twenty-five years, your wealth grows exponentially."

Twenty-five years? Ash reflected. That was a big chunk of time, but then all of his get-rich-quick schemes had flopped. He resolved to learn all he could from the Fellowship and to commit himself to the programme.

"In the beginning, you won't have much spare cash, but after twenty-five years, your Money Fountain will be flowing strongly. You will be set for a comfortable life and retirement and your children will be free."

Then he politely cleared his throat again, took a sip of tea, and crossed his legs.

"The first secret of the Money Fountain is to pay yourself first, 10 percent of your salary."

"How do I do that?" asked Ash.

"In order to pay yourself first, you have to get a job and create the initial flow of money. From this comes your 10 percent, and this will become the source of your Money Fountain."

"Yes," said Ash.

"The first few years will be tough, but if you stick to the plan and work hard, you will become wealthy. No matter how much or little you earn, you will become financially independent. All it takes is commitment and patience."

Ash nodded and silently committed himself to follow the teaching.

"In order to save 10 percent of your take-home pay, you have to create a budget. And in order to construct a budget, you have to understand income."

Ash nodded. He felt he understood income, but he was mistaken.

"Do you know that not all the money you earn is yours to keep?" enquired Dr Swan.

"I disagree with you," said Ash, shaking his head. "If I have worked for my money, it is mine to keep and mine to spend as I see fit."

"I understand what you are saying," said Dr Swan. "However, this approach will keep you enslaved. Blowing all your cash will never make you wealthy. Look at it this way. Not everybody earns the same amount, yet they are all equally broke. Why?"

Ash scratched around inside his head looking for an answer, but none came to his rescue.

"I don't know. Why?"

"People get confused between what they call necessary expenses and desires. Desires always match, and often exceed, your income. In order to satisfy desire, more money is often required. The confusion between necessary expenses and desires keeps people trapped in a cycle of poverty, and they are forced to work just to keep their heads above water. They go to work so that they can afford the things that they desire even though these desires keep them enslaved. People who are seduced by desires never get away from zero in the bank and often fall into debt by borrowing to maintain their lifestyles."

Ash had to admit this was true.

"The first step to freeing yourself from this wilful enslavement is to understand the difference between necessary expenses and desires. Can you tell me the difference?"

Ash had never thought about this and could not answer.

"Necessary expenses," said Dr Swan, "are things you need in order to survive and generate an income. Desires are things you don't need but want. Desires are illusions placed before you by advertisers."

Ash swallowed. He had never thought about it like this.

"Advertisers are paid to create desire, and they are skilled at their craft." Taking another sip of his tea, Dr Swan shifted to a more comfortable position. "Now, what are necessary expenses?"

Ash was sure he had a good idea what they were but deferred to Dr Swan with a shrug. This strategy did not work. Dr Swan would not allow Ash to shirk the question and gave him a piercing look that demanded an answer.

"Er, enough to eat," stammered Ash. "A warm dry home, love, family, warm clothes, an education, money to get to work."

"Good," said Dr Swan. "You are getting the idea. What you need to survive is basic and anything more is too much. But this 'too much' is vitally important."

"Why?" asked Ash curiously?

"Because you will create your Money Fountain from this excess. Do you understand?"

"Yes." Ash nodded.

"So," said Dr Swan, "pay yourself first. How do you do this?"

Ash was unsure.

"Your take-home pay is the money you receive in your bank account after the government has taxed your salary."

Ash was unsure what Dr Swan meant, and Dr Swan noticed.

"When you analyse your payslip, you will notice that the government takes the first cut without even asking you; and the more you earn, the more they take. This is a mandatory tax on your earnings. What remains of your salary is referred to as your take-home pay.

"Now divide this money into ten equal portions. If you are going to save the first 10 percent, then do exactly what 'pay yourself first' means. Create a stop order or direct debit and pay that money into an account *first* before making other payments," said Dr Swan emphatically. "That's what 'pay yourself first' means. This is vital. It's non-negotiable."

Ash nodded. This was serious.

"Now, you need to adjust your expenses so that you can live comfortably on the remaining 90 percent."

"Like cutting your pattern to suit your cloth," said Ash.

"Correct!" Dr Swan nodded and continued. "But is the remaining 90 percent yours to keep?"

"Sounds like no," said Ash.

"You're right," said Dr Swan. "The taxman is still not done with you. Almost all the products you buy attract Value-Added Tax (VAT), so the government takes another percentage of your hard-earned income. In some instances, like imported goods and fuel, the government takes even more. Your take-home pay has just shrunk again, but at least you have a choice over what you buy and can limit the ravages of VAT. And then there is the 'silent destroyer.'"

"The silent destroyer?" asked Ash, a little exasperated. "What's that?"

"Inflation; it reduces the value of your income every year."

"Oh!" said Ash, surprised. This was news to him.

"So you receive your net pay minus the government's first bite and VAT's second bite. Is what is left yours to keep?" asked Dr Swan.

"I am not sure," said Ash. "Sounds like 'no' again."

"Unfortunately, you are right again," said Dr Swan apologetically. "You still have more commitments. You need to look after your family. You need to pay your rent, medical aid, electricity, phone, clothing, and food. You need to buy fuel and maintain your car. You might have insurance premiums and car repayments. There will be other hidden expenses, and this is before you start entertaining yourself."

Ash was feeling pale.

"To be honest, there is a lot of pressure on your take-home pay, and sadly those expenses are rising faster than your pay is increasing," said Dr Swan. "But this can be offset by enjoying work, working hard, and studying."

This was a light at the end of the tunnel. Ash felt relieved.

"If I understand correctly, you have succeeded in saving 10 percent of your take-home pay but lost your savings twice, I think, on dodgy investments?"

"Yes," said Ash, blushing.

"I believe your wife took the slipper to you."

"Yes."

"Good. Have you learnt your lesson?"

"Yes, I have." Ash nodded. His surrender was complete.

"So, in order to save 10 percent of your take-home pay, make a detailed list of all your needs and expenses. Then identify the essentials and drop the rest. You may need to sell some things and absorb the knock, but you have to set a budget that works on 90 percent of your take-home pay. Do not try to grow your income first. This will not work. First save 10 percent of your current income. Fail here and your Money Fountain will never work. Do you understand?"

Ash heard that loud and clear.

"The next step is to grow your income. This is how you offset inflation. Work hard and enjoy your work. Become an expert in what you do. Study. But don't study only because you want to increase your pay, study so that you can become wiser. Learn more about the world. This cultivates your power and improves your confidence. This will make the Goddess feel more comfortable being around you, and as her trust in you begins to grow, so things will start to go your way. Remember, it is the Goddess who opens doors that lead to new opportunities; respect and honour her."

"Excuse me, but how come you also refer to the Goddess of Luck?"

"Yes," said Dr Swan. "She plays an active role in everybody's life. She has brought the Fellowship together and made it work. It seems to be her intention to change how money flows around the world, and she has chosen you to be a mentor, Ash. But before that, there are many hard yards. You need to be focussed."

Not wanting to get diverted from his purpose, Dr Swan continued. "The next step is to address your debt. If you have debts, settle these as quickly as possible."

Ash swallowed. He understood debt well.

"The Goddess notices debt, particularly bad debt, and she finds this offensive. Debt affects your confidence."

"How?" asked Ash curiously?

"Instead of being relaxed and assertive, you retreat at moments when you should be forthcoming. Others notice this, as so does the Goddess."

Ash nodded. He was keen to build his relationship with the Goddess.

"You manage your debt by using two-tenths of your take-home pay."

Ash looked confused, and Dr Swan noticed.

"Put all your debts in one pile and divide it by the number of your debtors. Next contact all of your debtors and inform them that you will be paying them all equally. This is your debt plan. Some will get angry and others will demand to be paid first, but stick to your guns. The Goddess will notice this and be well pleased."

Ash swallowed again.

"Now that you have saved 10 percent and are spending a further 20 percent on repaying your debts, how much are you left with?"

"Seventy percent."

"Good lad. Now this means cutting your expenses even further, but you got yourself into this mess and only you can resolve this matter. But don't fret; once your new budget starts to work, everything will be much brighter. The Goddess will also be impressed and come closer to you. Good luck will begin to come your way.

"Most importantly," said Dr Swan, sitting forwards and waving his hands as if he were about to crash. "Avoid more debt at all costs. This is a priority.

"It's quite easy to understand how people are seduced into buying things that are not essentials but desires. And once people get into debt, they have to pay interest on their loans, and that is exactly the position the lenders want the borrower to be in."

"A credit card is the most ingenious method to enslave people. It is a honey trap set to entice you into its web, where it plans to keep you. If you use a credit card, you will be paying a high interest rate on your unpaid balance. This is another way in which your hard-earned cash drains away from you and into the hands of others," said Dr Swan with scorn.

"If a credit card was called what it actually is, a *debt* card, fewer people would use it," said Dr Swan. "And the bigger your debt, the harder you have to work. So let's think smart; let's turn that around and make you a winner. Let's make your money work for you and not you for it."

Ash was keen to know more about how money could work for him as he was getting a little tired of working for it.

"It is important," continued Dr Swan, "to recognise the havoc desire plays in your life. Desire confuses you. It presents itself as real, but this is the honey in the advertisers' trap. They are trying to entice you into buying something they have been employed to sell. It's like giving a thirsty person salt water to drink. It's a drink designed to make that person thirstier, and the advertiser gets rewarded for encouraging you into the honey/buying trap."

"How is the advertiser rewarded?"

"He or she gets paid for the job."

Ash got the idea. As he looked out of the window, he saw a butterfly dancing among the roses.

"The advertisers' message is seldom designed to empower, though it is dressed up as if it were so intended. How do they do this?"

Ash had never understood this dark craft.

"Advertisers create your insecurity by comparing you to their, so to speak, perfect role model. Their message appeals directly to your desire to be wanted and successful."

Ash understood the downside of vanity.

"But we have logic," continued Dr Swan, "and can think our way through this problem. If you wish to create a Money Fountain, you will need to apply your logical mind."

The butterfly flew back to the window.

"Our Fellowship promotes conscious wealth, meaning you have to rise above yourself and use the power of logic. Disciplining the mind is essential to saving, and without being able to recognise how you are seduced by desire, you will remain a slave."

Ash had never thought of himself as a slave, but he seemed to be one stuck on a treadmill of desire.

"Your failure to recognise the power of desire also has an enormous impact on the environment."

"How so?" asked Ash.

"Because, according to the WWF, every kilogram of stuff you acquire generates thirty-two kilograms of waste. This is the primary cause of environmental destruction."

Ash saw a mountain of rubbish and was shocked by the waste.

"At this stage, it's important that you start to recognise Mammon, the god of greed," continued Dr Swan. "He is a fallen angel, a dark lord who has come to rule the world. He is very real, and people commit abhorrent crimes in his name every day."

Ash didn't understand.

"Since people first began cultivating crops, they have merely refined the processes by which they exploit the environment. This they call progress, and they celebrate it. They have turned capitalists into role models, and in this frenzied pursuit of money, some people commit unspeakable cruelty to animals and the environment."

In a voice tinged with regret, Dr Swan said, "Mammon has come to dominate most people's lives to such an extent that they now use money and their debt as a measuring stick for their success. But this is an illusion because you can't eat money. Neither will it bring happiness, only loneliness and suspicion. This is spiritual poverty, which is a deep sense of alienation, a syndrome where life loses its value and meaning. The aim of the Fellowship is to turn this around and create a mechanism that generates wealth and is beneficial to the environment."

Dr Swan took a few moments to compose himself.

Ash looked out of the window. He now understood that if he was to become financially independent, he needed to rise above himself and recognise the consequences of his desires. He was making excellent progress, and the Goddess had good reason to be pleased with him.

"So, to summarise: 10 percent saved, 20 percent for debt, cut your pattern to suit your cloth. No other way," said Dr Swan. "Get rid of your credit cards. If you have debt, you start with a handicap, so address this matter as soon as possible."

Then Dr Swan looked Ash straight in the eye. "Do you get my point?"

"Very clearly."

"Good. It's non-negotiable. Get this wrong then DCM."

"DCM?" asked Ash.

"Yes. DCM. Don't come Monday."

Dr Swan cleared his throat and continued. "And DRB."

"DRB?" asked Ash.

"Don't rent, buy."

"Do you mean I should buy my own home?"

"Yes," said Dr Swan.

"But I will need to take a loan, and you advise against that."

"In this instance, and in this instance alone, we advise you to borrow the money."

"Why?" asked Ash.

"If you rent all your life, when you retire, you will have nothing to show for your efforts. But logic can prevail, and you can turn this loan to your advantage."

"How?" enquired Ash.

"First, buy a solid home in a modest area, and then pay off more than you have to. This will save you a fortune, but remember, always pay yourself first."

Ash was not completely sure how taking a loan to buy a house could work for him.

"Many people who live in expensive houses don't actually own them, the lending agency does," said Dr Swan, chuckling to himself again. "The highest percentage of people who actually own their own homes live in the poorer areas."

Then he gazed into the distance and thought for a while.

"There's a lovely story about Elvis Presley," said Dr Swan, chuckling. "When he first moved into Graceland, the neighbours weren't at all thrilled and wanted him to move. Their ire was focussed on Elvis's washing that was being hung up outside. So they called a neighbourhood meeting at which they hoped to draw up a petition. But when the meeting opened, the bank manager reminded them that Elvis was the only one who had actually paid for his house. The meeting closed promptly."

Ash laughed. He understood.

"The point is that in the rich areas, the bank owns most of the houses. This is not wealth; it's just a façade, a boost for the ego. In truth, these people are Mammon's slaves working to pay the interest on their loans, and thereby providing the source of Mammon's Money Fountain. The higher your expenses, the harder you have to work. Get it?"

Ash got it.

"When you own your home, you are wealthy, and it doesn't matter where that home is; your cost of living drops. So when it comes to buying a home, it is wise to buy in a modest area. And as I said, in this case, it is okay to borrow the money. In this instance, and this instance only, debt can work for you."

"How?" asked Ash.

"If you pay off more than your scheduled monthly payments, you will save a small fortune in interest payments. Do this and the Goddess will be very happy with you."

Ash nodded. This made sense.

"Security is also an integral part of the operating system of paying yourself first."

Ash thought about burglar bars, but Dr Swan soon dispatched this vision.

"Wealth needs and clings to protection, and this makes the Goddess much more comfortable. So take out life insurance and make a will. When you do this, the Goddess will relax. The butterfly settles, so to speak."

Ash did not understand, and Dr Swan noticed. "If you are unsure about anything, speak to TK. He will arrange for a tutor."

Ash made a mental note.

"Should you unexpectedly pass away, life insurance and your will are designed to protect your family. Life insurance also covers you in the case of disability and protects your other investments, like your home and car. But don't buy a car on credit. That's plain vanity. The purpose of a car is to get you from A to B, not to attract a mate."

Ash clearly understood the downside of flashy cars.

Dr Swan stared into the distance for a while, trying to conjure up a suitable example to illustrate the importance of his point on protection. Finally, he settled on walls.

"In ancient times, walls offered good insurance from marauding armies," he said. "Take Babylon, for instance. It was a large city in the Middle East built on the plains between two rivers. It was not on a trade route, it did not have mountains, a port, or forests, yet it was fabled for its wealth and Hanging Gardens."

"How come?" enquired Ash.

"All Babylon had going for it was water, good soil, and the labour of its citizens. The farmers made profits and paid taxes, which the city elders invested in strong walls that offered protection from attack. When invading armies did attack, the farmers simply retreated behind their walls and waited for the attackers to run out of steam. Eventually, unable to breach the walls and because armies are expensive to maintain, the invaders packed up and went home. When the coast was clear, the farmers emerged, repaired their lands, and continued producing. In this way, Babylon's walls were their insurance and the secret to their success. In the same way, you need to use insurance to protect your family's future and the fruits of your labour."

Ash nodded.

"That's really it," said Dr Swan. "That's the nuts and bolts of the pay-yourself-first secret. Save 10 percent of your take-home pay, trim your expenses, settle your debts, protect your investments, and buy a home. Get these in place and you are on your way to creating your Money Fountain. When are you going to start?"

"Today," said Ash. He now understood that he alone was in control of his desires and destiny.

Dr Swan smiled. "Once you have managed to get your budget under control, the next hurdle is how and where to invest."

"The million-dollar question," said Ash.

"Not so. It's simple. Big Julius and Mrs Blumkin will explain the ins and outs to you. Remember, a fool and his money are soon parted. As you well know, there are countless stories of people who have been seduced by get-rich-quick schemes, only to be taken for a ride."

Ash felt his embarrassment tapping him on the shoulder but as he had acknowledged his mistakes, he had no cause to feel like this. He had learnt from experience and had reason to be proud.

Two more butterflies joined the first and together they flitted through the garden. Ash thought of the Garden of Eden. The advice hinted at a possible return.

At this moment, the Goddess intervened and caused young Ms Swan, who had been lounging at the poolside, to become uncomfortable, so uncomfortable that she needed to come inside and interrupt the teaching.

"Sure is shapely," commented Dr Swan as the young lady approached. Once again, she swished her tail in a feline manner, and then she came directly to the point; she wanted to go out for lunch. Now.

"I'm busy, love," said Dr Swan. "Can we go a little later?"

"But I'm hungry now," purred Ms Swan.

Dr Swan melted. "Good. Ten minutes?"

"Please excuse me," said Dr Swan to Ash. "Duty calls."

Ash journal entry 21.11.2012

Pay yourself first. No shortcuts. Turn 1 rand into R5 625 in 25 years…so that means R1 000 will become R5 283 000. Sounds even better. Pay yourself first=save 10 percent of take-home pay…difference between income and take-home pay=tax. Establish difference between essential and desirable expenditure and the temptation dangled by advertisers. I think I get that. Set a new budget that fits 9/10 of take-home pay. Cut desires from expense account. Desire leads to financial slavery…I agree. Build my confidence by studying…good idea. Enjoy work… can do. Check with TK re: life insurance and wills: IMPORTANT. *Good debt and bad debt…pay off debt as managed priority…use 2/10 of take-home pay… Ouch…Fair call…I made the mess…have to clean it up myself.* IMPORTANT! *Don't get into more debt…return credit cards ASAP…debt card. What a grand idea. Buy own home in a modest area…cheaper…I agree. Thank you, Goddess… You have changed my life for the better.*

CHAPTER 6
sHARk

The venue TK had chosen was an outdoor restaurant on Fish Hoek beach that was famous for the wrong reasons. A great white shark patrolled the shore and had already devoured a few swimmers. Strangely, the beast always left a calling card: sometimes a bathing cap, sometimes a pair of goggles, and sometimes a limb. Much to the public's horror, not only was the shark comfortable dining in broad daylight, it was also happy cruising the shallows just beyond the breakers, where bathers could see it.

Once again, Ash had to cross the railway tracks, but this time depression did not accompany him. He was early because he liked being early and chose to sit on one of the brightly coloured benches with a view across the bay. After ordering a cappuccino, he sat back and took in the view over the beach, through the bathers, past the shark, and across the bay to the distant purple Hottentots Holland Mountains, where the sun rose. The sun was out, and only a few puffy clouds drifted across the sky. The beach was bustling with many young mums who had brought their children to enjoy the fine weather. While there were many families on the beach, Ash noticed that only a few bathers ventured into the water and some never ventured beyond the level of their knees. When a wave altered this ratio, the bathers retreated quickly.

When his coffee arrived, Ash noted that the foam had bubbles and did not support the weight of the sugar. The milk had obviously been heated to more than 63°C. Ash wondered about TK's preference for outdoor eating establishments; they usually seemed so down market.

The train whistle brought Ash back to the moment. When he looked around, he saw TK.

"What is it with you?" laughed Ash as TK seated himself. "The coffee here is terrible."

TK smiled, appreciating Ash's observation. He was wearing a business power suit: an open-neck white shirt with a dark sports jacket. It was not possible to tell if TK was having a bad hair day because his bouffant had still not settled.

"I love the outdoors," he said, settling in. "It's our greatest wealth, and it's meant to be enjoyed. True wealth is to be found in your environment, not in your pocket."

The waitress approached the table and TK ordered a cappuccino.

When TK had first suggested that it was time for Ash to plan his passing, or crossing over, as TK preferred to call it, Ash had visions of dull thuds on a wooden box and worms and maggots. He also had visions of himself standing before the good Lord and having to explain his misdemeanours.

"No, no," said TK. "This part of your education focusses on protecting your gains. Today I do not want you to think about your mortality. Rather, I want you to plan for it."

"Not a pleasant topic." Ash swallowed. Maybe the coffee wasn't that awful.

"But essential."

"Why today?"

"Because this should have been done yesterday," said TK. "If you procrastinate any longer, all your hard work may have been in vain."

"How so?" asked Ash.

"Because if you die without a will, the state will settle your estate. This process could take years, it costs a lot, and, most importantly, you will lose the flow of your Money Fountain; it will be choked off by legality."

"But I won't be here," said Ash.

"But your family will," said TK sharply. "And that is why you need to plan for the event."

The sharp rebuke focussed Ash's thoughts.

"If you cross over without a will, your family will be left in a financial crisis."

Ash felt the blood drain from his head. He went pale. All his hard work and sacrifice would have been in vain, and this was plain stupid.

"I understand. Let's get down to business."

At this moment, TK's coffee arrived. He looked at it questioningly. "Foam's awful, but it's a beautiful day and we are alive. Cheers, young man. Here's to your Money Fountain!"

"Thank you," said Ash, raising his cappuccino. "I wonder why outdoor establishments often produce such substandard fare?"

"I don't know," said TK. "Maybe it's a message about priorities. What is really important? Coffee is coffee; some good, some bad. But look over there." He pointed to the mothers on the beach. "There's love. That's what life is all about—love and protection."

TK noticed a grey strand in Ash's mop of dark hair. "What's that? A grey hair?" he asked, touching Ash's temple.

"Can we stay focussed," smiled Ash, pushing TK's hand away.

"Okay, okay. We are meeting today because Dr Swan reported that you did not understand the protection aspect of the Money Fountain. This is a session to focus on protection and security, and I will fill in those gaps for you, but you will need to see professionals to implement the process."

"Understood," said Ash.

"Life insurance and wills are two essential aspects of the Money Fountain. Like the walls of Babylon, they offer you protection and security, both of which financial wealth needs. Without these, the Goddess will never be comfortable at your side."

Having come to know how the Goddess had altered his path, Ash was keen to please her. He actively sought to grow and cement their relationship. Protection was a key point he had missed during his wandering years, and he knew that it was time to stop procrastinating.

"When you start on the road to creating wealth, you need to ensure that your gains are secured. You may not always need life insurance, but you will always need a will," said TK.

"Protection comes in the form of different insurances that one needs at different times in one's life. When you have a young family and new home, you need to insure your life and debts. These priorities will change in your midlife and retirement. Protecting your family is a structured programme, and, as you will see, an essential element of the ongoing functioning of your Money Fountain. Remember, the true beneficiaries of your Money Fountain will be your children and grandchildren.

"The rationale behind your investment and insurance must be your will. It determines how your assets will be distributed when you die. This event is inevitable, so why not plan for it now?"

Ash agreed. Push had come to shove.

"Making a will gives you peace of mind. It removes that 'what if' nagging feeling from the equation. Once you have drawn up a will and resolved your insurance, you will feel lighter immediately," said TK, taking a sip of his coffee. "But if you die without a will, you are considered intestate."

"What's that?" interrupted Ash.

TK ran his fingers through his hair as he realised the extent of his task.

"It means you have crossed over without a will. In that case, the state takes control of your assets and it decides how they will be distributed. Your estate will be frozen immediately, and the court winds up your estate. This is a protracted process and could take years and cost a lot," said TK, sounding ominous.

"Your debts will be settled first, and any legal fees related to a court case will be paid before your family will see a cent. The court will then distribute the remaining monies according to a set of rules. Your family will be the biggest loser, and only because you failed to draw up this simple document."

Ash felt a pain in his stomach and moved to ease the discomfort. He was unprotected, and therefore, so was his family. He now realised this was short sighted.

"And because your debts are paid first, your family loses the lump sum that life insurance pays out. This money could have been invested and your debts paid from the dividends."

"In the same way that debtors are paid out of two-tenths of income?" asked Ash.

"Yes," confirmed TK.

Ash swallowed. He was staring into the looking glass of reality.

"Not making a will is short sighted and silly. Besides, it only takes a few hours to draw it up. While the service is free, there are hidden costs, but I will come to those."

"I am getting this," said Ash, nodding.

"Even if you are in prime health, you have no way of knowing when the bell will toll for you."

"Point taken," said Ash. "I will see to it immediately."

"In your will, you will nominate your beneficiaries. You might also choose to set conditions as to how your assets will be managed. Your will is your opportunity to plan this."

"How do I make a will?" asked Ash.

"Well, it's best to consult a professional, but enquire about the costs first. These are key. Some lawyers and organisations will take up to 7 percent of your estate. They might also charge for attending meetings and phone calls. This is why they usually offer to draw up your will for free, and some don't mention the clause related to their charges. If a bank draws up your will, they'll most probably nominate themselves as executors, so it is best to approach your family lawyer and confirm a locked-off fee."

TK continued. "There are a couple of other basics about a will. It must be signed at the end by you, the testator, dated, and witnessed by at least two competent witnesses, neither of whom can be beneficiaries. And please note, if you get divorced and you don't change your will within three months, your ex still inherits."

"Got it. What is a testator?"

"A testator is you, the person who writes the will. *Testate* means having left a legally valid will."

The waitress interrupted and asked if they intended eating. Neither was sure. More clouds had gathered in the sky, momentarily pinching the sun.

"Before you go and see your lawyer, map out what your estate consists of," TK continued. "That means you need to list your assets and who the beneficiaries are. You also need to spell out how your assets are to be distributed. Most importantly, you need to nominate your executors."

"Executors! What do they do?"

Again TK ran his hand through his hair and gazed into the distance, seeking patience. When he found it, he sighed and continued.

"An executor's job is to make sure your assets are distributed and managed according to your wishes. He or she is the person who is going to manage your family's future. You need to choose this person or persons or institution carefully, and then nominate him or her in your will."

Ash scratched his head. This was more complex than he'd expected.

"When you nominate an executor, choose a family member or friend. Your executor will have to attend quite a few meetings, so choose somebody you can trust and who lives nearby. An executor should also have money-management skills, be honest and reliable, and have your family's best interests at heart. Just in case the person you nominate either can't, or is unwilling to be your executor, nominate an alternative."

Ash's heart sank.

Noticing Ash's concerned look, TK tidied up. "It is also a good idea to choose somebody who will probably outlive you, so an aging parent might not be a great idea. This is why nominating an alternative person is a good idea."

"Yes. Got that."

"Part of an executor's job is to collect all the monies owed to you and pay your debts. He or she has to file all the proper tax documents, distribute your estate, and more. This is not an easy task, so think carefully about who you will entrust this responsibility to."

Ash nodded. He was regretting not having brought his notepad.

"Your will is like a shark net. It is designed to keep the sharks out. To do that, it needs to be scrutinized regularly. Make sure your executors know where to find your will and that you have an updated net-worth statement."

"A what?" asked Ash, exasperated? These were complexities he had never dreamt of.

TK laughed. Patience was now firmly seated beside him, and together they took the long view. TK had also been in this position.

"A net-worth statement records all your assets. Assets are things you own. Your net-worth statement also records your debts—money you owe. When you subtract your debts from your assets, you get your net worth," said TK, looking at Ash to see if he understood.

Ash nodded.

"Let us hope you own more than you owe. This is where insurance is vital. Wills and insurance are important to maintain the flow of your Money Fountain. Smartly managed, it can grow on its own."

'I am getting there,' reflected Ash.

"If your will and net-worth statement are up to date, winding up your estate should be simple. This is for the benefit of your beneficiaries. These are basic rules. Get them right."

"Right," said Ash, though he was a little unsure. TK saw this.

"When we next meet, you need to give me proof you have begun this process or this fountain of knowledge will dry up."

"Fair call," said Ash, looking at the mountains in the distance. He was beginning to feel hungry.

"Not making a will is a needless mistake. Do I have your word that you will see to this immediately?"

"Yes," said Ash.

"A few years ago, the council was going to install shark nets, but this has never happened," said TK. "This procrastination could cost people their lives."

Ash now understood the need for action, and TK felt happy enough to continue with his revelations.

"So, now that you have a will, you need to start protecting yourself, your family, and their future. So let's talk about insurance. Remember, both the Goddess and wealth require security before they feel comfortable enough to grow."

"Why do people buy life insurance?" asked Ash.

"So that when they cross over, their family will have money to live on," said TK. "But there are many more aspects to insurance. You will need different insurances at different times. When your Money Fountain begins to flow strongly, you might not need it, but while still enslaved it is vital."

Ash took a sip of his cooling coffee and realised that he was still enslaved.

"How do you work out how much money your family will need?" prodded TK.

"I have absolutely no idea," said Ash.

"When you die, your insurance must be able to pay off all your outstanding debts, like your mortgage, your car payments, funeral costs, and winding up any business issues. Then it must also be able to provide living expenses for your wife and children and their education. This will require a once-off lump sum that can be invested. But please make sure that you include an additional 10 percent that can be invested in a compounding fund."

"What's that?" asked Ash impatiently.

"Patience, young man, patience. That will all be explained in good time. We are setting up the operating system. Do you understand?"

Ash nodded. He had much to do. TK was revealing how unprepared he was to manage a Money Fountain.

"In order to work out how much cash your surviving spouse and children will need, you will need to attach values to this sum. When you have done that, add an additional figure to protect against inflation."

"And the 10 percent for the Money Fountain," said Ash.

"Sounds complicated, doesn't it," said TK. "Once you have established your family's financial needs, start approaching insurance companies about life insurance. Do some research and check out several policies before you choose one, and be sure to read the fine print before you sign any agreement. Ask as many questions as you need to, no matter how stupid they might seem to you. Enquire about fees and charges and get the figures in writing. If you don't understand, don't sign."

"I understand," said Ash. His coffee, like his appetite, had cooled. The sun appeared from behind the clouds and brought warmth. The kids on the beach made more noise.

"There are two types of insurance," said TK. "Short and long term. Short term covers assets such as cars, home mortgages, and the contents of your home. Long-term insurance covers your life and retirement. For the purposes of today, and while we are discussing your will, I am only going to discuss long-term life insurance. This is for protecting your family and your retirement, remember.

"Short-term insurance is something you will need to work out for yourself, but the less you spend, the more money you have to invest in your Money Fountain. Capiche?"

"Absolutely."

A ball came bouncing past the table with two little boys chasing after it. Having found it, they fled in a flurry of noise.

"The point is," TK continued, "that you only need life insurance when you have people that rely on your income. If you are single and don't have any kids, then you most probably won't need it; but if you have debts like a home mortgage, then you do. If you are married and have children, as you do, then you definitely need this cover."

Ash nodded. He had a family.

"When establishing how much cash your family will need, it is wise to factor in inflation. This will be the number one enemy of your beneficiaries. Inflation's eroding power is relentless. Because your beneficiaries will be living off the dividends of your savings, the compounding power of your wealth will be reduced by inflation's creep. That's why it is important to instruct your executors to provide for the 10 percent compounding facility so that your Money Fountain continues to grow."

"Do I need to insure my children?"

"No. They are liabilities."

"Liabilities. How?"

"In this instance, children are a liability because they cost you money. If they cross over, they will leave a massive emotional gap in your life, but your expenses will drop. In the broader sense of the word, a liability is a debt for which you are responsible, so in a way a child is a liability because you have an obligation to finance their education and lifestyle until they are independent."

"Is my wife a liability?"

"If a spouse does not work, you could see it that way. But if she is a homemaker, rearing your family, she is an asset and you may want to insure her life. For instance, if your wife suddenly crosses over, you, the surviving partner, are going to have to cope with a lot more than her sudden departure. There are millions of things house mums do that are unseen and unappreciated. So, in the ideal world, you will want to insure your wife's life for the total of your combined debts, including the mortgage on your house. This is a good idea because a debt-free balance sheet greatly reduces the stress on a suddenly single parent. There will be other costs like funeral expenses, day care, and babysitters. You are going to need more money than you suspect, so plan for the event."

Ash was going pale.

"Put some more sugar in your coffee," directed TK.

"Why?"

"You are losing focus!"

TK waited while Ash poured another sachet of sugar into his cold coffee and stirred it. After taking a sip, his colour returned.

"Your life insurance should also make provision for the event that both you and your partner cross over within a short space of each other and leave your child an orphan."

"What a horrid thought."

"I agree," said TK. "It might sound morbid at this moment, but believe me, your survivors will be much more confident when they are standing next to your coffin if they know that you have been brave enough to face and resolve these issues."

"I suppose so," said Ash, watching the children playing on the beach. A few boys were making mud balls and hurling them at each other. The mother swooped and, scolding them, put a swift end to the game. The boys objected loudly, but their attention soon drifted to the water's edge.

"If you are in a business with somebody, should you insure them as well?" enquired TK.

"Why would I want to do that?" replied Ash, shifting around, feeling uncomfortable.

"That wasn't a trick question," said TK. "Should you insure a business partner?"

Ash had no idea.

"The reason you should insure your business partner is that if he or she dies, the person's net-worth statement will list your business partnership as an asset, and you could soon have a new business partner with new ideas. If you insure your business partner, you will be able to buy that person's shares and not have to worry about a new business partner. This could also apply to other assets like house and tax liabilities you bought shares in with friends and family."

"What are tax liabilities?"

"This is money you might owe the taxman. Look at it this way," said TK, fumbling for an example. "Imagine that you have done well and invested your windfall in several properties. These are financed through loans and rental agreements. But you get taken out. Because of the size of your estate, your executors receive a large tax bill, which has been levied on your estate. Estate tax only applies if your estate is worth more than a certain amount, but your estate is worth a lot more. If you had not insured these investments, your executors may be forced to sell some of your properties to cover the tax bill. If you had evaluated your tax liability correctly, you could have insured this as well."

"All of this insurance is going to cost a lot," said Ash.

"Not really," said TK. "It is part of the cost of running a business and must be included in any business plan."

Watching the kids playing at the water's edge, Ash realised that life insurance was more complex than he could possibly have expected. He also realised how important it was. TK left Ash with his thoughts and had some coffee. Then he picked up the trail and continued.

"When you fill in a life insurance policy, your broker will ask you to name a beneficiary. At this moment be careful," said TK, "because you need to state who the executors of your estate are. If you name your beneficiaries, the insurance company will pay the money straight to them. This will affect your Money Fountain and defeat your carefully planned investment strategy."

"What is the difference between an executor and a beneficiary?" asked Ash.

"An executor, as I have told you, is the person who is responsible for the administering and winding up a deceased's estate, and a beneficiary is the person or people who benefit from your will."

"Will I get a payment when my life insurance policy matures?" enquired Ash.

"Not necessarily," replied TK. "There are two types of life insurance: cash value and term insurance. Cash value is life insurance with a forced savings component, which you will receive when the policy matures. Term insurance is when the policy expires, so does the insurance. There is no savings or investment element. Term insurance is cheaper because it doesn't have the savings component, but if you are the custodian of a Money Fountain, then you can invest the difference in your Money Fountain."

Again the clouds borrowed the sun's warmth. The excitement on the shore calmed.

"The reason insurance companies sell cash-value policies is that the monthly premiums and agents' fees are higher. In practice, cash value is usually the better option because people tend to spend the extra cash on desires. But you are different, Ash, because you are conscious and have the discipline to save 10 percent, which you are investing in a compounding facility, so you don't need cash-value insurance. But you still need to insure your debts."

"Why?" asked Ash.

"Because you have debts," said TK. "But when these are paid off and your Money Fountain has a healthy flow, you might not need any life insurance. Plan your net-worth statement in such a way that should you die, your survivors will emerge cash-flow positive. Your aim should be to free them from financial insecurity and give them the best possible shot at living a happy, complete life."

Ash took another sip of coffee. He felt like he was being examined under a microscope and found wanting.

"When you retire, the premiums on your life insurance might rise as well. To prevent this from happening, find a life insurance policy that allows you to renew the policy when the term expires at the same premium."

Ash nodded.

"Shop around for the best deals. Life insurance policies are a lot like cans of baked beans. There are many different brands, but only one might suit your needs. Be assertive; ask difficult questions."

TK pondered. "Tell me, Ash, you aren't planning on departing soon, are you?" he asked.

"Not quite yet." Ash smiled. "To be honest, I am really beginning to enjoy my life, and I am looking forward to creating my Money Fountain."

"Good," said TK. "So you are planning on living into old age?"

"God willing."

"If that's the case, then what are you doing about your retirement?"

"What?" asked Ash, incredulous that another challenge had popped up on the horizon?

"Retirement. When you finish working and go out to pasture. Have you made provision for that?"

"Nope."

Their gaze drifted onto an old couple struggling up the beach towards the restaurant, both poorly clothed and unkempt. Ash saw himself and acknowledged the warning.

"The reason most senior citizens live in or close to poverty is because they haven't planned properly. A retirement plan is essential for a comfortable old age, and this is where most people come unstuck. When they retire, their income drops and they are required to make lifestyle adjustments. Some of these changes can be big. In the last ten years of your working life, your cost of living will drop. You will have paid off your home and furnished it. Your kids should have left home. As a result, you may have more spare cash. What are you going to do with this?"

The old couple made it off the beach and sat down at a table. The waitress approached them with menus. They studied these briefly and then ordered filter coffee. TK noticed. He called the waitress over.

"Please offer them breakfast. Whatever they want and bring the bill to me."

She did as instructed. The couple looked over at TK and thanked him and reopened their menus.

Returning to the topic, TK said, "This extra cash should be pumped into your Money Fountain. When you retire and are no longer earning a salary, your income drops dramatically, and if you haven't planned for this, your standard of living could drop. Adjusting to this will be a challenge. The best advice I can give you is to start preparing for your retirement now. This is the primary purpose of the Money Fountain. Your retirement plan should be sufficient to provide for you until the day you die. This is the strength of our philosophy, and if you start early, it will make you wealthy without all the stress."

Confusion did not leave Ash. "Your time with Big Julius is just around the corner," added TK.

TK left Ash to himself for a while and enjoyed the view. By and by, Ash found himself and resurfaced to find a contented TK enjoying the warm sunlight. It was time for Ash to ask TK a question. "Why do you refer to death as crossing over?"

"That's soul talk. If you like, we can pursue the matter of your soul at a later point," said TK and returned to the business at hand, setting up Ash's next tutorial.

"When you get your will and life insurance policies in order, it will be time for you to learn about the Magic Penny. This is a job for Big Julius. He lives near Coffee Bay in the Eastern Cape. When you get to Coffee Bay, ask the first person you meet how to get to Big Julius and he will take you there."

As Ash left TK and the beach, his head was spinning. It seemed as if a new era of security and calm was being ushered into his life, and he was attracted to it like a moth to a lamp on a moonless night.

Ash's journal entry 28.11.2012

Fish Hoek Beach, sharks, crap coffee. Thank you, TK. The image in the mirror becomes clearer. Need life insurance, but needs to change as I age. Will sets out how my assets will be distributed. Intestate=dying without a will. NOT GOOD. *State resolves my will…will pay debts and lawyers' fees first…family gets what is left and loses control over lump sum, which could have been used to pay debts using the 2/10 formula.*

Will—must consult a professional. NOTE: *See charges and costs. Executors implement provisions in the will, pay all taxes, etc. Executors need to be honest, reliable, live close by, and be good with money. Nominate an alternative. Net-worth statement… list all assets and debts (value=total assets less debts). Tell executors where will is and lodge net-worth statement with it. Good idea! Executors collect all monies owed and pay debt.* IMPORTANT: *Debts can be settled from 2/10.*

Life insurance. How much will Suraya need? Must cover debts and maintain family. Add 10 percent for future investments and component for inflation, banking fees, and costs.

Short- and long-term insurance. Short term covers mortgage and cars. Long term covers life insurance…maybe Money Fountain covers this: check with TK. Insure

Suraya for total of debts, day care, and babysitters. Don't insure kids. Plan for in case both mum and I are killed together (horrid thought). Insure business partner and tax liabilities…an excellent idea…if you have a business partner.

Life insurance: two types. Cash value insures life with forced saving component. Might not be necessary if I am investing 10 percent in Money Fountain? Term insurance. Cover will cease when policy matures, company might load new fees. Seek a policy that addresses this.

Plan for retirement. TK suggests Money Fountain might do the trick…am not so sure. Many questions.

Chapter 7
Big Julius

Having planned his journey and bought the tickets, Ash found himself on a bus travelling through the rolling green hills of the Eastern Cape heading for Coffee Bay. It was not an air-conditioned luxury bus, but it was a warm, fun bus. Destiny found Ash seated among some old women and men, children, sacks of corn, chickens, two goats, and a piglet. It smelt like Africa and Ash liked it.

They spent the morning driving over and around hills, passing small congregations of mud and thatch-roofed huts, occasional cultivated fields, roaming cattle, and through many potholes. Now and then, the bus stopped and somebody got off or on, but never at a bus stop. There were no fences, and dogs didn't bother chasing the bus.

At midday, the bus arrived at a trading store perched on the edge of an escarpment. From here the land sloped down to the coast, and Ash could see the Hole-in-the-Wall, a unique headland of rock rising straight out of the ocean. Cut off from the land, it stood like a stubborn slice of toast, its top crowned with rocky peaks and dense bush. In its middle, worn through by the waves, was an archway. When the sea was rough, the waves burst violently through the hole.

Without fanfare, the bus driver closed the doors and drove on, plunging into the forest. In the early afternoon, the bus arrived in Coffee Bay, and Ash prepared to follow TK's instructions. He was the last person to get off at the last bus stop—the beach—and the first person he met was a young herd boy who was watching his cows lazing on the beach.

"Hello," said Ash. "I'm looking for Big Julius. Do you know where I can find him?"

The young herd boy looked Ash over with curiosity. *Could this bloke be the famous rugby star? No.* He dismissed the thought. *That guy would have been in a flashy car.*

"Sure," said the boy. "It's too late to go now. I can take you tomorrow. We must walk. Okay? I will see you here, at this spot on the beach, at sunrise."

"How far is it?" asked Ash.

"A long way."

"What's your name?"

"Vuyo."

"How much will you charge to take me to Big Julius?"

"One hundred rand."

"Okay," said Ash. "Where should I stay?"

"The hotel over there," said Vuyo, pointing at a big white building. "I will meet you at this place at sunrise tomorrow morning. Bring hat."

The cold grey light of dawn found Ash standing on the beach looking out to sea as the first orange blush of the rising sun brushed the horizon. Ash felt at peace with himself. His relationship with the Goddess was going well, and he was grateful that she was making the pieces of the puzzle fall into their correct order and place. Ash realised how much easier life is when you have a guide, and he began to look forward to his future with confidence. He closed his eyes in prayer. When he opened them, an orange line on the horizon had grown into a glowing ball and Vuyo was standing next to him.

"It's sunrise," said Vuyo. "We go. Yes?"

"Good morning," said Ash.

"You pay me now," said Vuyo, holding out both hands.

Ash handed over a new one-hundred-rand Madiba note.

"When will we get there?" asked Ash, but Vuyo had already started walking and was out of earshot.

Grabbing his day pack, Ash set off after Vuyo, who set a cracking pace. Ash would have to step on it if he hoped to keep up. The path led to the end of the beach and then climbed over a hill. From the crest, it plunged down into a milkwood forest and reemerged on a beach littered with boulders. A short way off the coast stood the majestic cliffs of the Hole-in-the-Wall. Ash was awed.

A large pool opened out in front of the mouth of the Hole-in-the-Wall. It was replenished by the waves crashing through the hole and a river running down from the escarpment, forming a perfect swimming pool.

"We cross here," said Vuyo, pointing to a narrow sand bar that ran under the water. Then he pointed to the sea just beyond and said, "Over there, sharks."

As Ash struggled with his shoes, he was rapidly becoming aware of just how much of the country boy still lived in him. He, like Vuyo, was happy barefoot. He put his trainers in his pack, shouldered it, entered the pool behind Vuyo, and waded across the sand bar. When they emerged from the pool, Vuyo was waiting for Ash. Pointing to a path running along the riverbank, he said, "This path takes us to Big Julius. Long way!"

The path led inland along the riverbank for half an hour and then came to a fork; one side led along the riverbank, the other into the forest. A cluster of butterflies swarmed around the entrance to the forest, and Ash had to pass through them.

"Hello, butterflies," said Ash, standing with his arms outstretched as if he were showering in butterflies. Recognising the presence of the Goddess, he entered the forest with confidence.

The path climbed steadily all morning, twisting around the contours of hills. They passed many small compounds of mud and thatch huts set in fields of cultivated corn. Unseen voices called out, and though Ash could not understand what was being said, Vuyo responded with something that always included *Big Julius* in it.

Vuyo walked quickly and seldom waited for Ash. Late in the morning, while climbing along the edge of a precipice, they came to a break in the forest. Across the valley, Ash saw a waterfall of remarkable beauty, but Vuyo had little time for the view and continued hiking. After another two-hour hike, they emerged on a rock platform high above the forest.

"We take a break here," said Vuyo, pointing to the rocks.

Ash was pleased for the break because his thirst was killing him. Scratching around in his pack, he produced two bottles of water, one of which he gave to Vuyo. Then he produced a packet of white-bread polony sandwiches wrapped in greaseproof paper. He gave half to Vuyo.

Ash noticed that every time he handed Vuyo a gift, he always clapped his wrists together twice and then accepted the gift with both hands, bowed his head, and said, "*Enkosi (Thank you)*."

Ash then produced a jar of pickles. He liked pickled onions with polony sandwiches. He picked out a big onion with his fork and passed it to Vuyo. Having finished his sandwiches surprisingly quickly, Vuyo examined the onion and Ash with equal portions of curiosity and mistrust. Then he cautiously tasted the onion with his tongue. It sprang back.

"No, no. You must bite it like this," said Ash, biting his onion in half.

Vuyo did as Ash suggested, but he had not anticipated just how strong a pickled onion could be. His face contorted as a massive sneeze took hold, with the tart pickle juice whizzing around inside his nasal cavity, tickling it until tears streamed from his eyes. Then, like a tennis ball reaching the zenith of its flight, the sneeze floated up and hung there for that exquisite moment, unsure whether to subside or unleash its fury. Quite peculiarly, Vuyo took control of his malaise by stretching out his lips like a leopard stretches when it awakens, thus relieving the sneeze.

It took Vuyo a few minutes to return to himself, and when he did, he straightened out his jacket, wiped away his tears, and passed the second half of the onion back to Ash.

"Thank you," said Vuyo, "but I don't like this onion."

After lunch, they continued the climb on the path through the forest and, as if as payback for the pickled onion, Vuyo set a cracking pace again and raced ahead of Ash. Late in the afternoon, they emerged below a cluster of huts in a clearing on the edge of an escarpment.

"Big Julius lives here," said Vuyo. "I am going now."

"What do you mean? How will I get back?"

"They will sort it out."

By now, Ash had begun to understand the ways of the Goddess and accepted each new revelation as it was intended.

"Good-bye," said Vuyo, raising his hand in farewell. "You nice guy, but I not like pickles."

"Thank you and goodbye, my friend," said Ash, feeling forlorn. But he spoke to the wind, as Vuyo had already melted back into the forest.

Alone, Ash turned to climb the last few steps. He had been walking and climbing for the best part of eight hours. He was exhausted and sweaty and his knees ached, but he was pleased that his hamstring had survived the ordeal.

Taking a deep breath, he climbed the last few steps and emerged in a compound with five mud huts painted rich chocolate brown. They were set in a semicircle around a central courtyard, surrounded by a low retaining wall. A large mango tree grew in the centre of the courtyard with a half circle of benches set under its shade. Ash imagined that this was the tree of knowledge where the elders gathered for their *indaba*, their tribal council. A three-legged pot stood bubbling over the fire, smoke drifting across the courtyard. It smelt of Africa and filled Ash with a sense of his roots. Coming home. Growing.

"Hello," called Ash.

Nobody answered, so Ash waited a few moments and then called out again.

"Wait!" a voice cried out. Ash couldn't determine from where.

The door of the hut next to the cooking fire opened, and a very sleepy maiden emerged rubbing her eyes and yawning.

"Hello," said Ash. "I've come to see Big Julius."

"Who?"

"Big Julius."

"No." She shook her head. "No Big Julius here."

"What do you mean?"

"No Big Julius here."

"I don't understand. There must be some mistake. I've just walked the whole way from Coffee Bay to see Big Julius and you tell me there's no Big Julius?"

"Sorry." She looked about her. "Big Julius? No, sorry. I don't know him."

"Vuyo brought me here to see him!" said Ash, close to exasperation.

The young lady looked at Ash with suspicion.

"Did you pay Vuyo?"

"Yes," said Ash.

"Nah," she laughed. "You got taken."

Ash felt his blood pressure rising.

"Vuyo does this all the time," continued the young lady. "We have many visitors like you. I don't know why."

"I don't believe you," said Ash.

Exasperation had by now blanketed Ash. He could feel that swear words were not far away.

"Do you even know Big Julius?" said Ash, his fury growing.

"*Hayi (Excuse me)*. No. Sorry. If you have walked the whole way and Vuyo has taken your money, then I am sorry for you. *Yho*, that Vuyo," she said, shaking her head.

At that moment, a new voice entered the courtyard.

"Molly! Molly! Stop that immediately."

Ash hit the bottom of the rabbit hole with a bump.

An elderly dark-skinned man in a white linen suit appeared from behind the last hut and then gingerly made his way down the slope with the aid of a walking stick. He was a short, thin man with grey hair and round spectacles.

When he made it into the courtyard, he approached Ash directly.

"Are you Ash?"

"Yes," said Ash, feeling relieved.

"TK said you might arrive today."

"Are you Big Julius?"

"Yes and no," said the old man, smiling.

"Don't believe him," shouted the girl. "He always pretends to be Big Julius."

Ash found himself lost in a maze of Alice in Wonderland proportions. To be fair, it was actually the Goddess who was most thrilled by the events she had inspired, but Ash couldn't see her.

Pouring oil on troubled waters, the old man interrupted. "Let me start at the beginning. First, I apologise about Molly; she gets a kick out of watching visitors' faces."

"Don't believe him!" shouted Molly. "He always does this."

"*Tula (Quiet)*, Molly," said the old man firmly. "I am Big Julius, but I am not. Big Julius is a nickname. You, young man, may call me Julius."

When Ash landed on his feet, he found himself freshly showered and standing alone in a large room with a magnificent view over the escarpment, forest, and ocean. He noted the laptop and mobile phone on the polished desk.

"Do you like the view?" asked Big Julius as he entered the room behind Ash.

"Yes, indeed."

"Would you like a gin and tonic?"

"Thank you," said Ash, "but I don't touch alcohol."

"Each to his own." Big Julius invited Ash to be seated. "What can I get you?"

"A cup of sweet tea would be fabulous," said Ash.

Taking Ash by the arm, he led him to a leather couch scattered with white silk cushions. The room reminded Ash of Dr Swan's lounge.

"I'm pleased you like my setup," said Julius. "Did you know it's entirely off grid? We work off solar power, biogas, and wind. But the wind's not that consistent here, so we depend mostly on solar and biogas."

"That's impressive."

"Thank you," said Big Julius, smiling. "I enjoy being in nature, and it's so much more peaceful. With modern technology, I can run my business from here just as if I was in the city, and I get to enjoy the splendour of nature and the environment. Living in such luxury would cost a fortune in the city. Here, I save a small fortune."

Ash liked the music as well, but didn't know that the mellow crooning voice was that of Chet Baker, singing something about "everything happens to me."

Ash noted the serendipitous nature of the moment the Goddess had arranged to reveal her presence.

When Ash was comfortable, Big Julius pressed a buzzer next to him. "Molly, please bring Mr Ash a cup of tea. I will have my usual."

"Isn't it a bit early?" asked the voice over the intercom.

"That will be all," said Big Julius, turning to Ash. "I believe you have met with Dr Swan?"

"Yes."

"Nice chap. How did that go?"

"Well, thank you," said Ash, still adjusting to his day.

"Tell me about your discussions."

"Dr Swan revealed the operating system of the first secret—pay yourself first. We spoke about a Money Fountain that can turn R1 into R5 625 in twenty-five years. TK mentioned that you would reveal the secret of the Magic Penny to me. He also said that I should speak with Mrs Rose Blumkin after I have consulted with you and that she would reveal the third secret."

At this moment, Molly arrived with the tea and a drink for Big Julius.

Much to Ash's relief, Molly was now properly attired. She gave Ash his tea, stood back, and looked him directly in the eye. Then she winked and smiled.

"You are looking much more comfortable now, Mr Ash. Did you enjoy your shower?"

"Thank you," said Ash warily. He was unsure if he liked or trusted Molly.

"One and a half sugars?"

"Thank you."

"Loser," said Molly with a smile as she left the room.

Ash, feeling thoroughly uprooted, waited for Molly to depart before continuing. He did not notice, but the door did not click shut.

"Dr Swan taught me about the importance of paying yourself first and the difference between essentials and desires. He also explained how advertisers use temptation to get one into debt. Since our meeting, I have learnt about life insurance and am in the process of drawing up a will. On my journey, I have come to recognise the hand of the Goddess, and it seems we are learning to get along. I am merely a pilgrim on the path of life."

"You are doing well, Ash; one of our better students."

"I assume you are also a follower of the Goddess of Good Luck? I would really like to know more about the Fellowship."

"I am indeed," said Big Julius, "and will gladly enlighten you. She is our patron. She introduces new students to the Fellowship. There is no vow or covenant that binds the mentors and tutors other than their word that they will pay it forward. We were shown the secrets and are bound, indeed happy, to share our knowledge with those whom the Goddess introduces to us. Our mission is conscious wealth."

"Yes, TK spoke about this, and I am keen to know more about conscious wealth."

"All in good time," said Big Julius. "Mrs Blumkin will introduce you to that."

Then Big Julius switched the conversation. "Have you ever heard the 'Tale of the Magic Penny'?"

"No," replied Ash.

"It's straight arithmetic. Are you any good at maths?"

"Not really," said Ash, taking a sip of tea.

"That's not a problem," said Big Julius, taking a sip of his drink. "You don't have to be good at maths to create a Money Fountain. You only have to be consistent."

Big Julius's gaze drifted out of the window as he summoned the story.

"Say, for instance, I were to offer you a choice between taking three million rand in cash and a single cent that doubles in value every day for thirty-one days. Which would you choose?"

"The three million rand, of course," said Ash without hesitation.

"Most people would. But you have made the wrong choice," said Big Julius. "The cent that doubles in value will lead to greater wealth."

"I don't believe you."

"Choosing the Magic Penny route takes much longer to see the reward, but it's been tested," said Big Julius. "It just takes dedication, time, and patience to turn R1 into R5 625, as Dr Swan promised."

"I'm not sure I believe you," said Ash.

"Okay," said Big Julius. "You take the cold hard three million rand and your friend goes the Magic Penny route. On day five, your friend will only have sixteen cents, while you will have three million rand, which you are spending. On day ten, your friend will only have 5.12 cents. How do you think your friend will be feeling about his choice while he watches you spending your millions?"

"Most probably not happy," conceded Ash.

"After twenty days, your friend's penny has grown to R5 243. How is he feeling about his choice now? Hopefully he has done the maths and is delighted. But let us suppose he has not done the maths. Jealousy and regret may have raised their heads. You, on the other hand, are enjoying what's left of your three million."

Ash remained alert, though sceptical. Aware of the Goddess's flair for practical jokes, he was on his guard.

"But then the tide turns," said Big Julius. "Just a little at first, but the flow that has been doubling in size every day now begins to quicken. Eventually, your friend's river of money turns into a torrent, and the single cent that doubles every day now starts to grow rapidly. On day twenty-nine, when you've got what's left of your three million rand, your friend's cent has grown to be worth R2.7 million. So you now begin to doubt the wisdom of your decision. On day thirty, your friend pulls ahead with R5.3 million. On day thirty-one, on the very last day, your friend ends up with more than R10.5 million. On day thirty-two, his Magic Penny will again double, giving him twenty-odd million. Thereafter, his money doubles every day. This is the invisible magic of the compounding effect."

Ash sat in disbelief. Could this be the source of the Money Fountain? His enthusiasm rose.

"Now, how does that compare to your three million? If you are feeling like a greedy fool, you are right. This is the secret to compound interest and the Money Fountain's engine. Do you now understand how, if you keep investing your 10 percent and reinvest your dividend, your wealth grows faster and faster?"

It was as though Ash had been slapped again. He began to see through the mirror to what was on the other side.

"Few things are as impressive as the magic of compound interest," said Big Julius. "You generate earnings from previous earnings. This is the way that money works for you and not you for it."

"I am not sure I understand you completely," said Ash.

Ash looked out of the window and across the valley and lush forest. In his mind, he saw a Money Fountain, but this one had a silver lining.

"The best way for your money to grow," said Big Julius, taking a sip of his drink, "is to invest in something that has a reasonable growth rate linked to the compounding factor, like a share on the stock market, where your investment grows and you earn dividends as well. The magic comes when you reinvest your dividend. This is how you generate earnings from previous earnings."

Ash still did not quite understand, and Big Julius noticed.

"If, for example, you invested R100 in a company and earned a 20 percent return, at the end of the first year, you would have R120. The next year, you would earn 20 percent on your R120. The following year, you would earn 20 percent on your R144, and so, year after year, your money grows. In this manner, the compounding effect opens a cash stream that multiplies exponentially. At first, the flow will be a trickle, but every month the trickle will grow until it becomes a torrent. The trick is to start. That's why saving 10 percent of your income is the key. You have to start now."

Ash still had misgivings.

"Come, let me show you," said Big Julius. Picking up his drink, he led Ash out the door and up the hill. Below them was the cattle enclosure.

"For example, it's like those cows in the field," said Big Julius, pointing to his herd of cattle. "In the first year, a cow produces one calf. In the second year, you will have two cows that will produce two calves. In the third year, you will have four cows that will produce four calves. If all goes well and you manage to protect your herd and they produce females, in the fourth year, you should have eight cows that produce eight calves. By the sixth year, you should have thirty-two cows that produce thirty-two calves. The growth curve is exponential. This is the reason why the old African economy was based on cattle. Even if the female is not pregnant, she still has the potential to produce. This is the compounding principle. But cows also produce males, and they get sick and die, so you need to find a facility or instrument that is constant and secure."

Ash began to understand.

Smiling, Big Julius turned to Ash and said, "Money doesn't work quite the same as cows in the field. Money doesn't face the same threats, but it does have risk. The secret is to reduce risk and costs, thereby maximising your return. But I think you get the idea."

"I do," said Ash enthusiastically, finally getting the point.

"The principle of the Magic Penny is the driving force behind the Money Fountain. When you can establish at what rate your money grows, you can work out how much money you will earn. You do this by applying Rule 72."

"Rule 72?" asked Ash.

"Rule 72 gives you an indication as to how long it takes for your money to double."

Ash didn't get it.

"Assuming that your money grows at 15 percent a year, divide 15 into 72 and you get 4.8 years. That's how long it will take your money to double."

Ash scratched his head.

"Let's take another example," said Big Julius. "Say your money earns 12 percent interest per year, divide 12 into 72 and you get six years. If you can find a facility that offers you 30 percent, then your cash doubles in a little over two years."

This blew Ash away, and immediately the ultimate secret clicked into reality. "But what should I invest my money in?" asked Ash.

"That's a subject for Mrs Blumkin. That's her strong suit," said Big Julius. "You have much to learn, young man, so take your time and let the information sink in. I will inform TK about the gaps."

As they walked back to the homestead, Big Julius put his arm around Ash and said, "Having followed the advice of the Fellowship, I am now enjoying the sunset of my career. I am living off the fruits of my Money Fountain, which is still growing. As you can see, we are comfortable and we are enjoying the finer things in life."

"And the huts down below?" asked Ash.

"My wives live in the compound," said Big Julius.

"You have wives?" asked Ash, aghast.

"In traditional custom, I have three wives. Under European law, I have three girlfriends."

"Is Molly a …?"

"No. She works here."

"Oh."

"Say, old chap. Do you have a car?"

By now, Ash had learnt the ways of the Goddess and replied honestly, "Yes and no."

"I don't understand," said Big Julius.

"I own a car, but I came by bus. Why?"

"Oh," said Big Julius, thinking for a while. "You could have driven up here. How are you going to get home?"

"Vuyo said you would see to that."

"Oh. In that case would you like to stay for dinner?"

"Thank you. But I'm not sure how I'll get back to my hotel."

"Oh. Don't worry, old chap. Molly will run you down after dinner?"

Ash's journal entry 4.12.2012

Big Julius. What a trip, what a dude. The Magic Penny, who would have thought that money could be set to work for the individual, not the individual working for money. Now to invest my 10 percent in a facility that compounds, but where to find? Will check with TK. Must say, sounds fabulous! My Money Fountain begins to take shape. One secret to go…and what of conscious wealth?

CHAPTER 8
RAY ABRAHAMS

TK soon received word of the deficits Big Julius had detected, and because there was no sense in Ash meeting Mrs Blumkin before he understood how a stock exchange works, he set about rectifying the situation. A new tutor, the irreverent Mr Ray Abrahams, was appointed to the task. The meeting was set to take place at Olympia Bakery in Kalk Bay. TK hoped that this venue would staunch Ash's constant comments about poor coffee.

From the outset, it was obvious to Ash that Mr Abrahams was different. He was young, good-looking, and had a flair for the alternative. He was dressed in a charcoal suit with a thin charcoal tie and a white cotton shirt. His black hair was combed neatly backwards and he sported a diamond earring in his left ear. Had Ash known it, he might have thought he was talking to one of the Blues Brothers, but he didn't, so this moment also sailed straight past him. Ray was relaxed and charming, with a hint of naughty thrown in. His smile fizzed with humour and delight bounced in his eyes. Judging by what seemed to be Ray's roving eye, it seemed to Ash that Mr Abrahams was single and played the field.

Ash was also soon to discover that Mr Abrahams did not beat around the bush either.

"TK tells me that you think Wall Street is a temple of greed," said Ray in his opening salvo.

"I've heard it called that," admitted Ash.

"Do you know what a stock market is and how it works?"

"Not really, no."

"That's what TK said," replied Ray, smiling. "How's your coffee?"

"It's great," said Ash above the din of the busy coffee shop. Indeed, Olympia's coffee was good. This signalled a change. Here the foam on his cappuccino was thick enough to support the weight of the sugar. *The milk must be under 63°C,* thought Ash.

"Have you tried their almond croissants?" asked Ray.

"I haven't."

"You've gotta. Olympia makes the best almond croissants."

"You're different, Mr Abrahams," said Ash.

"Different, how?"

"We usually go to venues that make terrible coffee."

Ray laughed. He enjoyed being petted.

"There is a time and place for everything," said Ray with an offhand smile. Then he beckoned to the waitress, who came over.

"An almond croissant for my friend, please."

Ash noticed her good looks and smiled. The Goddess was back.

Ray got straight to the point. "Do you know how a stock exchange works and what a stockbroker is and does?"

Ash honestly did not know and looked forward to being tutored.

"Let's start at the very beginning. I am going to teach you about a stock exchange and how it works. Mrs Blumkin will teach you how money flows through the economy and what to invest in. She will also explain how to generate wealth that is good for the environment."

"Sweet," said Ash, nodding.

The waitress returned and placed before Ash a large almond croissant dusted with icing sugar. It looked fabulous. When Ash looked up, he looked straight into the waitress's eyes, which sparkled and flashed.

"Ah, the Goddess." Ash smiled to himself.

"You know her?" enquired Ray jealously.

"Yes, I do." Ash smiled, confidently holding his own. He now recognised temptation when it presented its charming profile. "The stock exchange; I am keen to be enlightened."

"Choice, young man, is always yours. I see you are making excellent progress."

Ash took a sip of his cappuccino. It was warm, silky, sweet, slightly bitter with a hint of chocolate and a dusting of cinnamon. There was only one sadness for Ash; with each sip he took, the beautiful heart the barista had created in the foam was distorting and was now long and thin.

"Imagine you want to open a coffee shop, but you don't have enough money to open your business. Where would you find the money?" asked Ray.

"The bank?" replied Ash tentatively.

"Maybe," said Ray, "but the bank won't lend you the cash if you don't have any assets to borrow against. So you have to find investors elsewhere. But where?"

Ash shrugged. This was unfamiliar territory.

"You could approach family members and friends or place an ad in the newspaper or online. But let's imagine that you are lucky and you find a few people who are prepared to lend you the cash. These people are called investors. When they lend you money, they are buying shares in your business. In return, you will pay the investors a proportional share of your profit. This is called a dividend."

Ash nodded.

"The reason people are willing to buy shares in a business is so that they can earn money without having to do any work," said Ray. "To do that, they need to have enough money to buy in. That is, to lend you. The money that investors lend to you is called their 'principal.'"

Ash nodded.

"When you saved up your 10 percent, you were saving up a principal. TK tells me you managed to do this twice, but both times you lost your savings. Is this correct?"

"Yes. I made mistakes. Big ones," said Ash, feeling embarrassed.

"People only learn from their mistakes. That is part of the journey."

The waitress came to serve the table next to theirs. As she caught Ash's eye again, he noticed her nostrils flare and realised the Goddess was tempting him again.

Ray smiled. He knew the game, and Ash was doing well. "Okay. Back to your coffee shop and investors. After a year, some of your investors want to sell their shares. Where would they find buyers?"

Ash shrugged his shoulders. He was used to earning a salary and saving, not finding investors.

"When raising money for new venture businesses, large and small, you face the same problems."

Ash was unsure what Ray meant.

"A business needs to raise money from people who have money, and people who have money to invest seek companies that pay a good dividend."

Ash nodded.

"A stock exchange is like your local supermarket that sells a wide variety of foods and other items, many of which are similar and competing brands," said Ray. "The reason people go to a supermarket is because it is convenient and they can do all their shopping in one place. A stock exchange is a supermarket for shares. Do you understand?"

Ash nodded.

"The stock market is a place where people who want to buy and sell shares gather," said Ray, confirming his point while taking a sip of coffee. "It is a legal market where the money you loan to a business is passed to the business. In return, investors get a share certificate."

Ash nodded again.

"Are you going to try your croissant?" asked Ray.

"Yes. Yes. I was listening to you."

"Well, let's eat and talk at the same time."

Ash nodded.

"Here," said Ray, "let me show you. Break off a piece of your croissant with your fingers and dunk it in your coffee like this." Ray dunked his bit, popped it into his mouth, and savoured the flavour. "The best part is licking your fingers afterwards," he said with a sparkle in his eyes.

Ash was finding the ride informative and enjoyable.

"So," said Ray, licking his fingers again. "A company wanting to raise money on the stock exchange will approach the stock exchange and request to be listed. Once the company has met the legal requirements set down by the stock exchange, it becomes a listed company. When a company becomes listed, it can legally sell shares in itself to the public. It will usually issue many millions of shares."

Ash got it. The mist was slowly clearing.

"When the stock exchange is open, traders buy or sell shares at the current market price for clients. That job used to be done by the guys shouting on the floor of the stock exchange, but they have now been replaced by electronic trading platforms. Nowadays, stockbrokers enter transactions directly via electronic trading platforms," said Ray.

Ash nodded. The picture was becoming clearer.

"This brings me back to the original question, 'What is a stockbroker?' Do you know?"

"I don't," replied Ash honestly.

"A stockbroker is a member of the stock exchange and is licensed to trade shares on behalf of clients. He or she is your link to the stock market. Part of the service offered by a stockbroker is to advise a client on which shares to buy, sell, or hold."

Ash nodded.

"But be warned," said Ray. "Stockbrokers have fees, commissions, and conditions. These fees vary from broker to broker and, if you are not careful, these costs will affect your profit, so choose wisely. The key remains the same; reduce the commission charged by the go-between and invest the savings. Rose will advise you."

"Rose?" said Ash, enjoying his croissant.

"Mrs Blumkin, if you prefer."

"Oh. Right," said Ash, breaking off a piece of his croissant and dunking it into his coffee. "How do I buy shares?" After asking the question, he popped the piece into his mouth and savoured the sweet almond and coffee flavour as it trickled through his mouth.

Ray noticed and waited for Ash to return to himself before continuing.

"You can also buy shares online, but if you don't feel confident to do so yourself, then a stockbroker will buy or sell shares on your behalf. That is if you have sufficient principal in your stockbroking account."

"Principal?" asked Ash, thinking about school.

"Your principal is your ten-percent saving."

Ash nodded.

"You can ask your stockbroker for advice, but remember advice costs. No matter what, the decision to buy and sell is always yours."

"It is also important to remember that when placing a trade over the phone with your stockbroker, your word is final," said Ray. "There is no written record of such instructions, and once the agreement is made, the exchange is complete. The trade is verbal and considered complete."

"Sounds dangerous to me," said Ash.

"The stockbroker's motto is *dictum meum pactum*," said Ray with a flourish. "It means 'my word is my bond.'"

Concern dashed across Ash's face. He had heard promises like this before, but Mr Abrahams moved quickly to allay his fears.

"If you like, you will be issued with a share certificate."

"That sounds better," said Ash, relaxing.

"This information is only a part of the rudimentary operating principles of the third secret. You are being tutored in this because we need to give you a clear picture of how money works."

Ray took another piece of croissant, dunked it, popped it into his mouth, and licked his fingers.

"The secret to the Money Fountain remains the same," he continued. "Save 10 percent of your take-home pay and invest in an instrument that compounds and rewards you either with interest or a dividend—the Fellowship advocates dividends. Please ask any questions that come to mind."

Ash kept quiet. When Ray gave him an enquiring look, he muttered, "Yes, and thank you. I will."

The look of concern did not leave Ash's face.

"You are right to be cautious about a verbal agreement, but a lot of money passes through a stock exchange every day. They know how to manage this process."

Ash accepted this at face value, but it was obvious to Ray that Ash was going to check up on this, and this was good.

"When a company wishes to raise money on the stock exchange, it goes through the legal process of getting listed. Once the company is listed, it becomes a publicly listed company and is then able to sell shares in itself."

Ash nodded.

"When you buy shares in a company, you are also entitled to attend the company's Annual General Meeting, vote members onto the board, and receive a dividend, if the company declares one."

"I don't understand how the price of a share is established."

The question impressed Ray, but sadly there was no simple explanation for Ash, though Mr Abrahams tried. "The initial pricing of a share is a complex process, but each share is given a price when it is first listed. The future value of that share depends on how well the company is doing and how many investors want to buy shares in it. This is called the share's 'market price.'"

Ash nodded.

"When a company makes a profit, that profit is divided by the number of shares it has sold, and each shareholder gets paid according to the number of shares owned. This pay-out is called a dividend. This is the money you receive for not doing any work. Right?"

"Understood."

"If the company does not make a profit, then you won't get a dividend and the value of your shares could drop."

Ash swallowed.

"But when a company does well, its shares become more valuable because more investors want to own them. When this happens, the share price goes up. This is known as capital growth."

"If a company is doing badly, people are inclined sell their shares. When there are more sellers than buyers, the market price of a share drops. This is a bad time to sell, but sometimes a good time to buy."

Ash nodded and took a sip of his coffee. Delicious. A bus drove past and shaded the restaurant; however, the hubbub in the room did not dim.

"The good news is that when a company loses money, you are not responsible for its losses. Your losses are limited to the price and the number of shares you own. It's not like a Ponzi scheme, where you lose all your money."

"Why did you say '*when* a company loses money'?" asked Ash.

"When?" said Ray, thinking. "Because all companies go through bad patches."

"Right," said Ash.

"Some investors buy and sell shares quickly, buying when shares are cheap and selling when the price rises. These investors are called speculators. This might sound like a good idea, but there are many reasons why this is not so."

"Why is that?" asked Ash. "It makes sense to me."

"Speculating is risky and stressful. You have to know the companies extremely well in order to choose the best shares to buy, and brokers charge fees and commissions that should be deducted from possible gains, so the more you speculate, the more costs you incur. Now, the more you limit these costs, the more money you have to invest in your Money Fountain."

Ash liked the sound of that.

"Speculators cause the share prices to rise and fall over a short period. This is known as 'volatility' and this scenario might not be in the investor's best interest. You with me?"

"Yes," said Ash, nodding.

"The Fellowship does not advocate speculation."

Ash got a warm, fuzzy feeling, as if he were being protected.

"So you need to find an investment that works for you. Mrs Blumkin will advise you about this. The aim of our Fellowship is to promote 'conscious wealth.' Have you heard of that?"

"Yes," said Ash, nodding.

Ray was tempted to start calling Ash "Noddy" but realised that Ash was a beginner and still nervous, so he let the urge pass.

"We seek to invest in companies that are environmentally friendly and have a social ethic, but I will leave that to your lessons on investments. My job is to explain the operating principles of the third and final secret. Are you with me?"

"Yes," said Ash, nodding.

"Remember, there are no stupid questions," said Ray. "If you have any questions, now is the time."

"Can a company issue new shares?"

"Yes. A listed company may issue new shares. This is referred to as a rights issue."

"Are all companies listed on the stock exchange?"

"No," said Ray. "A company that is not listed on the stock exchange is referred to as an 'unlisted company.' Unlisted companies also sell shares in themselves, but their shares are not protected or governed by the rules of the stock exchange."

"Would my coffee shop be an unlisted company?" asked Ash.

"Yes," said Ray. "This kind of investment might best be referred to as venture capital or private equity."

"When is it best to sell one's shares?" asked Ash.

"That is a job for Blumkin," said Ray. "The truth is that you can sell your shares whenever you wish to, but would that be wise? Selling negates the principle of the Magic Penny and will block the source of your Money Fountain."

Ash nodded. He was beginning to understand.

"We promote long-term investment, but any decision to sell your shares will always remain your right," said Ray, taking a sip of coffee.

Again, Ash nodded.

"So," said Ray, taking a long look at "Nodder" Ash. "You now know what a stock market is, what a broker is, and how to buy a share. You also know that each trade you make has a cost. You also know that companies seeking to raise money sell shares in themselves on the stock market."

"Yes."

"And you know that speculators can cause the share price to rise and fall."

"Yes."

"So how do you protect your investment against this volatility?"

"I don't know."

"You buy shares in many different companies," said Ray. "By not putting all your eggs in one basket, you protect yourself against the market's volatility. There is a very simple and easy way to do this, but Mrs Blumkin will tell you about that."

The picture inside Ash's head was becoming clearer. He was getting it.

"Finally," said Ray, with a big smile. "I think you are ready for Mrs Blumkin. I shall inform TK."

Ray took a break, eyed the waitress, and scooped up the menu.

"How about a drink and something to eat?"

"Sounds great," said Ash.

"Your shout."

"My shout?" asked Ash. "I don't understand."

"Oh," said Ray. "I don't have any cash on me right now. You don't mind getting the tab, do you?"

"No, no. Not at all," stammered Ash.

"Good. I'm famished."

The waitress, who had been watching the tutor and student while leaning on the display counter, almost choked on her chocolate brownie. She tried to hide this, but the spray of icing sugar in the air in front of her betrayed her. Ash didn't catch this moment, but Ray did; he was so loving this student.

Dusting off her apron, the waitress approached their table giggling.

"Everything all right?" teased Mr Abrahams.

"Everything is perfect," replied the waitress. "Are you ready to order?"

"I'll have a long Sauvignon Blanc with ice on the side and the mushroom linguine," said Ray, giving the waitress a wink.

She looked at Ash, who suddenly felt like that little boy on Dr Swan's couch.

"I'll have the same, thank you, without the wine. A glass of water for me. Thanks." The waitress noted their order and departed.

"You're married, right?" asked Ray casually.

"Yes," said Ash, retreating into his familiar pilgrim's habit. "We have one child and are expecting our second."

"Excellent," said Ray.

"Right. As far as operating principles go, there are some golden rules to investing. You'll probably forget some of them, but Mrs Blumkin will see you straight there," said Ray.

"Thank you," said Ash.

"Remember, be wary of investment gurus: nobody can predict the future. Take responsibility for your investments. Don't let your investments rule your life. You got that?"

"Yeah," said Ash. "I think so."

"If you have any doubts or questions, please feel free to call me," said Ray, handing Ash his card.

"Thank you," said Ash, nodding. "I will."

Ash's journal entry 8.12.2012

> *Ray. What a character. Coffee was great. Lunch was excellent. Stock market revealed. Didn't realise I knew so little. Seek investment that offers compounding facility—The Magic Penny.*

> *Ray's list of dos and don'ts (wonder if I can remember them all):*

> *Invest 10 percent of take-home pay…can do.*

> *Never go into debt in order to invest (good idea).*

> *Only invest money you don't need (right).*

> *Invest for the long term (fair).*

> *Reinvest your dividend (understood).*

> *Invest in quality (too poor to buy second hand).*

> *Buy shares that will grow.*

Stick to the basics (right).

Do not put all your eggs in one basket.

Check all the charges and make sure I understand them before I commit.

Be cautious of sages (yikes!).

Don't let your investments rule your life (big ask, but will try).

To bed now. I love my wife and daughter. God bless them, TK, the Fellowship, and the Goddess, without whom I would not be.

CHAPTER 9
MRs ROse BLUMKIN

Mrs Blumkin lived in a large colonial mansion that held a prime position at the Muizenberg end of Sunrise Beach, which curled round the bay and stretched as far as the eye could see, almost touching the Hottentots Holland Mountains, where the sun rose.

Ash felt good. He had climbed to the pinnacle of fame, lost it all, crawled through the murk of depression, and survived to find himself on the brink of a new pinnacle—financial liberation. Reflecting his optimistic mood, he was dressed in an open-neck candy-striped shirt and cream-coloured cotton slacks.

As he skipped up the stairs to the front door, a fresh breeze rustled the leaves of the palm trees. Water tinkled in the fountain and a sky-blue lotus flower bloomed in the pond.

He rang the front doorbell and turned to admire the view. Wow! A Christmas butterfly danced across the entrance. Once again, Ash recognised the presence of the Goddess and realised that temptation would not be far behind. He was not to be disappointed.

After a few minutes, a manservant in a tuxedo came to the door, opened it a crack, stuck out his head, and looked nervously at Ash.

"Is Mrs Blumkin in?" asked Ash in his best English.

"Heh?" said the manservant, cupping his hand to his ear as if to hear Ash better. "Come again?"

"Mrs Blumkin, please."

"Err, ma'am gone to town!"

"Mrs Blumkin," said Ash with a smile. "I have an appointment."

"No, sir. Ma'am. She in town."

"But this is the right address," Ash said confidently.

"Thank you," said Ash, smiling confidently. "But this is the right address."

Just then, a young woman with a dashing figure came up the stairs behind Ash.

"Moses. What are you doing?"

"Nothing, miss," said Moses, retreating. "The man wants to see Mrs Blumkin." "This gentleman has come to see Mrs Blumkin. Will you take him through?"

Ash smiled. The young lady introduced herself as Juliet and invited Ash to follow her.

She led Ash through the opulent foyer, which opened into a large dining room and flowed out through double doors onto a patio with yet another fountain. Ash would have been happy to linger in this room, but Juliet turned left and led him down a long corridor.

They came to a door and Juliet knocked. When there was no answer, she opened the door and invited Ash into a large study with bay windows overlooking False Bay. Two dark leather couches separated by a coffee table took up most of the floor space. A highly polished desk stood in front of the bay window at the far end of the room. Apart from a laptop and phone, the desk was empty.

"Mrs Blumkin will join you presently," said Juliet. "Please be seated." By the manner in which she indicated, Ash understood exactly where to sit, which he did.

Once seated, Ash looked around and admired the wood-panelled room. Like a library, it had extensive shelves filled with well-thumbed books. A large chandelier dominated the room. Hanging over a fireplace in the centre was an oil painting of a stern "blue" woman with bright red lips and a thick crop of black hair. She wore a beautiful ornate top rendered in gold, which shimmered in the light. Ash liked the top. The background was so rough that Ash thought it unfinished. He was fascinated by the woman's distant, removed, almost tranquil disposition. Ash liked the painting, but had no idea it was Tretchikoff's famous and highly sought-after "Miss Wong," sometimes called "The Blue Lady." Ash found the music playing gently in the background exquisite. It was the Adagio from Mozart's *Violin Concerto no. 3*. Ash missed this as well. He still needed much refining, but this rounding lay in the future.

Ash was still admiring the grandeur of the room and did not hear when Mrs Blumkin silently entered.

"You must be Ash," she said, extending her hand as she walked to greet him.

"Don't get up," she said, shaking his hand.

It was immediately obvious to Ash why the other members of the Fellowship referred to Mrs Blumkin with such deference. She was a no-nonsense person, though Ash suspected she had a warm heart and a sense of humour. She was short and stocky and stood solidly on her two feet, clad in dark shoes with a slight heel, wide and solid. She was old school, from an age when women "did" their own hair. Mrs Blumkin had done her hair with a perm and mauve rinse, which matched her mauve slack suit. She wore a double-string pearl necklace and earrings to match.

Ash suspected he was finally speaking with the oracle. He was.

"Yes," said Ash, standing up and shaking her hand. "Thank you for seeing me."

"The pleasure's all mine," said Mrs Blumkin, taking a seat opposite Ash. "TK tells me that you are ready to learn the third secret of the Money Fountain."

"I hope so," said Ash nervously.

"Would you like a drink?" she asked.

"That would be nice."

"What's your poison?"

"I don't drink alcohol," said Ash. "Water or tea would be wonderful."

Mrs Blumkin pushed a buzzer.

"Juliet."

"Yes, ma'am."

"Oh, Juliet. Will you please bring Mr Ash a nice cup of tea?"

"And for you, ma'am?"

"I'll have my sherry now. Thank you."

"Isn't it a bit early?"

"Thank you, Juliet. Now will be fine."

Then she turned to Ash and fixed him with her gaze.

"As he was growing up, to make money, Warren Buffett delivered newspapers, collected bottle tops, and sold peanuts and second-hand golf balls. In 1942, when he was twelve, he had already saved up a hundred and twenty dollars. In those days, that was a large sum of money, and he used it to buy shares in a company called Cities Services Preferred. He bought three for himself and, using her money, three for his sister Doris. The total cost to Warren was $114.75, meaning that each share cost $38.25. As luck would have it, the share price tanked, and within a short while, the value of the shares dropped to $27."

Mrs Blumkin cleared her throat with a polite cough.

"Every day, on their way to school, Doris reminded Warren that the value of her stock was falling. When the share price recovered to $40, Warren sold, netting them each a $5.25 profit. As if to prove a point, the price of Cities Services Preferred soared to $202 a share. In his rush to claim a quick profit, Warren had lost out on a potential profit of $490; a substantially bigger profit."

Again she cleared her throat.

"From this experience, Warren learnt three lessons he never forgot: don't overly fixate on the price paid for a share, don't rush in and grab a small profit, and don't invest other people's money because they can get upset with you. Warren learnt these lessons well and went on to become one of the richest people in the world."

Ash nodded, getting the point.

"These are some rules that apply to investing," continued Mrs Blumkin. "What is an ideal investment?"

"I have been trying to figure that out myself," said Ash.

"Well, the perfect investment is one where your money does all the work and you do none," said Mrs Blumkin. "This is what we mean when we say 'create a Money Fountain that will flow endlessly towards you.' But you can only achieve that when you get the basics of the operating systems in place."

She ticked them off on her fingers. "Job, 10 percent saved, 20 percent for debtors, own a modest house, write a will, take out life insurance, and get wise about advertisers. Got that?"

Ash nodded.

"And you now understand how the Magic Penny works."

"Yes."

"… and how the stock market works?"

"The basics, yes," replied Ash.

"This is good," said Mrs Blumkin. "And now you are ready to start investing?"

"Yes," said Ash.

"Wonderful. Once again, the team have done an excellent job."

Ash nodded.

A door at the far end of the study opened and Juliet entered.

"Juliet. Oh, Juliet. Have you met Mr Ash?"

"Yes, I have. We met on the steps. Good day, sir." She bowed her head to Ash.

"Your drinks, ma'am."

Juliet swung open the door and Moses stepped into the room carrying a silver tray. He approached the table and placed the drinks on it.

"Thank you, Moses."

Moses and Juliet retreated and closed the door behind them. It did not click shut.

"Right," said Mrs Blumkin. "You are now ready to learn the third and final secret of the Money Fountain—the ideal investment? What to invest in?"

"Yes. If you share your knowledge with me, you will not be a guru and you will bear less responsibility."

"Wise words," said Mrs Blumkin, "and I agree with you. So thank you. I will share with you, and I will share freely."

Once again, she cleared her throat.

"The shares we seek are those that grow by an average of 15 percent or more a year, pay regular dividends, have locked-in fees and no hidden costs, and offer you the choice to reinvest your dividend."

"Like the compounding effect of the Magic Penny," said Ash.

"Exactly," said Mrs Blumkin with a smile. "We also promote a long-term investment strategy of around twenty-five years, because the longer you leave your money in the market, the faster it grows."

"Is that a certainty?" enquired Ash.

"Virtually," said Mrs Blumkin. Then she continued. "So you have worked hard for your money. You have saved some cash and found a broker. You understand that brokers charge for their services, and you know how a stock market works. You are now ready to start investing."

"Yes, I am," said Ash enthusiastically.

"Do you understand the risk?"

"No," said Ash.

Mrs Blumkin looked at Ash and said *risk* softly to herself while studying the ceiling, as if she were calling up a file. After she'd located the file, she leaned forwards to pick up her sherry glass, and raising it, said "Cheers" before taking a sip. She did not put the glass down but delicately held onto it.

"The dictionary defines risk as 'the chance of something going wrong.' For convenience sake, I will try to make this simple for you."

"Thank you," said Ash. He was a connoisseur of simple.

"Compare the risk of investing to the risk of crossing a street."

Ash liked images. He found them easier to understand.

"When you cross a street, there is always a risk that you might get run over, so it's best to consider the different ways in which you can cross the street."

Ash nodded.

"Where you cross will depend on how fit and alert you are. If you are cautious or old and use a walking frame, then it's best to choose the safest options. If you are young and full of energy," said Mrs Blumkin, taking a larger sip of her sherry, "you might try a high-risk crossing, but there's a good chance you will get run over. If you do get run over, this will be your fault and you will have to suffer the consequences."

"Fair's fair," said Ash.

"Consider," said Mrs Blumkin, taking another sip, "that the flow of money through the economy is the busy street you are about to cross. You have arrived at the edge of this road of cash and now have to decide where to cross."

Ash nodded.

"In other words, you have to decide what to invest in."

The first thing you have been taught to do when crossing a street is to look left and right to see if there is any approaching traffic. This is like assessing your stockbroker."

She took a small sip of her sherry.

"The point at which you cross can be seen as selecting the kinds of shares you want to buy. There are conservative, medium-risk, high-risk, and just plain silly options. As you have been taught, the best place to cross a street is at a pedestrian crossing or traffic light where the traffic is regulated. Are you still with me?"

Ash nodded.

Mrs Blumkin finished her sherry. Then she leaned across and pressed the buzzer.

"Yes, ma'am?"

"Oh, Juliet. I've knocked over my sherry."

"Yes, ma'am."

"Right. Where were we?" said Mrs Blumkin. "Yes. That's right. Pressing the pedestrian crossing button and bringing all the traffic to a stop. It's safe, and if you do get run over, you will be covered by insurance. This is like leaving your money in a savings account in a bank. This will pay you a modest interest. It's a safe option, but if the inflation rate exceeds the interest rate, you will be worse off in the end."

Ash knew about the silent destroyer.

"You can cross the road when the traffic light is red and the green man is flashing. If you are fit and alert, then this is a relatively safe option. This could be considered to be an ETF."

"ETF? What's that?" asked Ash, realising this was the best time and place to cross the street.

"An Exchange-Traded Fund," said Mrs Blumkin. "But please be patient, I'll come to that."

Juliet appeared with the sherry decanter, recharged Mrs Blumkin's glass, and then took the decanter away.

"Thank you, Juliet," said Mrs Blumkin. "You can leave the decanter on the table."

"But …?"

"Thank you, Juliet. That will be all."

Juliet placed the decanter on the table and retreated. Again the door was left slightly ajar.

Taking up her glass, Mrs Blumkin continued. "You can always try and sneak across when the traffic light is green for oncoming traffic."

"This, of course, is only safe if you are fit and alert and can cross the street quickly. This is like the speculators who cause the market's volatility. This is stressful and if you get run over, it will be your fault," said Mrs Blumkin. "Alternatively, you can jaywalk and cross the road at any point. This is dangerous and could be considered venture capital, that is, investing in a new company without a track record. But those who invested in Apple shares will tell you this was worth the risk.

"The highest risk of all," continued Mrs Blumkin, taking a sip, "is to try to cross a road at night when you are drunk, wearing dark clothing, in a place where there are no street lights. You would agree that this is stupid, and you would only expect to find the unfortunate in this position. But believe you me, many big fish have been caught by this baited hook."

Ash laughed, recognising his folly.

"You might consider this high-risk crossing as an investment that offers returns that are too good to be true, like a pyramid or Ponzi scheme. These schemes promise fabulous returns, but they are illegal. Only those who get out early don't get burnt. If you want to throw your money away, then go for this option. I believe that you have had direct experience of a Ponzi scheme," said Mrs Blumkin, stealing a sip.

"Yes. That, and emeralds from Thailand," admitted Ash.

"I see," said Mrs Blumkin. "TK is well informed."

Ash cleared his throat and studied the painting above the fireplace.

"So, let's assess your best options. You might agree that crossing the street when the green man is flashing is the best option. There is a small risk, but it is generally safe. If something goes wrong, you have protection."

Ash agreed.

"Great. Now let's examine the performance of stock markets. On average, the stock market doubles in value every four and a half years. So if you invested

R1 000 in the stock market and left it there for twenty years, it would be worth R20 000. But if you invested R1 000 a month and adjust this payment annually to match inflation and, let's say, the average annual return on the investment is 15 percent per year, after twenty-five years, it would be worth R5 620 000, before costs."

Ash had a vague understanding of the Magic Penny, but this growth astounded him. He sat up.

"Over the entire twenty-five years, you will only have invested R662 000, and your investment will have grown by R4 620 000. This fabulous growth is achieved because you invested in an instrument that compounds, and you reinvested the dividend in that instrument. Even if you can only afford to invest a few hundred rand a month, you will still win. The reason for this is because the stock market is the ultimate arbiter."

"The ultimate arbiter?" asked Ash, thinking that this position was reserved for God.

"Everybody has an inbuilt fear of a stock market crash. Like people fear wildfire, they fear a stock market crash. This fear is based in the stock market crash of 1929. But when you apply logic, the 1929 stock market crash is not quite the train smash everybody makes it out to be."

"I don't understand," said Ash.

"If, for instance," said Mrs Blumkin, pausing for a sip, "in 1928, the year before the Wall Street crash, you had invested $10 000 in an index, ten years later, after the recovery had begun, your investment would have been worth $7 000. You would only have lost $3 000; not quite the catastrophe everybody made it out to be. But, if you had invested $100 a month over the same period and compounded your dividend, then your money would have grown to $15 000," said Mrs Blumkin, finishing her sherry.

Ash took a sip of his tea. Mrs Blumkin was making sense.

"Even though you would have invested $12 000 over the period, you would have endured the greatest stock market collapse of all time and still emerged with a $3 000 profit."

Ash did not seem impressed.

"The point I am making," said Mrs Blumkin, "is that in the long term, markets recover and grow. They have survived world wars, dot-com busts, housing bubbles, and credit crunch implosions. The stock market beats inflation and bank interest rates. We will speak about government bonds and mutual funds later. Juliet ..."

Juliet appeared around the door and hurried over to Mrs Blumkin, who held out the glass. Juliet refilled the glass.

"Thank you, Juliet," said Mrs Blumkin.

Juliet took the decanter and made to depart.

"Juliet. Please leave the decanter on the table."

Juliet hesitated, looked at Mrs Blumkin, and then did as instructed.

"The operating principle to making money on the stock exchange," continued Mrs Blumkin, "is to own as much of it as possible for as long as possible. Success can be explained by four factors: time, pay yourself first, invest in a compounding instrument, and reinvest your dividends in that instrument."

Ash nodded.

"Making money on the stock market is not about being clever and trying to outperform the market. In this way, you never stop running, and as you well know, one gets exhausted. In the end, worrying about the market will count against you. Also, don't put your faith in investment advisors or gurus. Over a six-year period, general global benchmark stock market indices, like the Dow

Jones, FTSE, Nikkei, JSE, and others, have outperformed those so-called advisors or gurus by nearly 50 percent. One of the reasons for this dismal performance by these so-called advisors or gurus can be attributed to commissions and fees that they charge clients. Fees required to pay analysts and portfolio managers to research and find companies that meet the portfolios mandate. In turn, fees and commissions erode performance. In essence, the various associated costs are eating up performance. Remember, they don't make their money from investments but from fees and commissions."

Mrs Blumkin continued, taking another large sip of sherry and nestling back into her chair, "Growing your wealth on the stock market is actually simple. The operating principle is owning shares in the biggest companies for as long as possible, even when the market fluctuates. Success is about how long you are in the market."

Ash nodded.

"And never speculate on the market," said Mrs Blumkin. "That's gambling. Occasionally, you might win, but in the long run, you will lose."

"I understand," said Ash, nodding.

"Another point," said Mrs Blumkin, "is that investors who constantly track the market and listen to the financial news actually often make half the money of those who pay no attention to it all."

This was a nice simple strategy, and simple appealed to Ash; a sound investment that worked on its own, just like a fountain should.

"Unit trusts, also known as mutual funds," continued Mrs Blumkin, "are not a great investment because their managers spend most of their time trying to outperform the market, but the vast majority end up doing worse; fees and commissions are the impediments to outperformance. Over a ten-year period, those that survived lag behind the market by 80 percent."

"Why is that?" asked Ash.

"Because their costs, fees, and commissions work against them," said Mrs Blumkin, taking a large sip before continuing. "The key principle to investing is 'don't be greedy.' Speculators buy and sell shares quickly in the hope of beating the market, and it is they who cause the market's volatility. But it is the big companies that cause the stock market to grow over the long term."

"It sounds a bit like flies buzzing around an elephant," said Ash.

"Yes," said Mrs Blumkin, smiling. "It's a bit like that."

"Successful investing relies on limiting costs. All investments have costs related to buying and selling shares, and there are fees for receiving advice. Brokers apply administration fees and they charge commissions. These fees are constant, regardless of what the market does."

Ash nodded.

"The rules of wealth are straightforward and simple," said Mrs Blumkin, listing them on her fingers. "Wealth multiplies happily for those who invest wisely, it needs and clings to protection, it abandons those who invest in businesses they know little about, it flees from those who are not skilled in working with it, and it shuns those who try to extract impossible returns from it, those with little or no experience in dealing with investments, and those who gamble. Without wisdom, wealth is easily lost."

Ash recognised many of these lessons from his own personal experience.

"When it comes to investments, the old adage, 'if it sounds too good to be true, it probably is' applies. Avoid pyramid schemes. Don't invest in businesses you know nothing about. Don't invest in a project where you will end up having to do the work yourself.

"But with wisdom," said Mrs Blumkin emphatically, "those who do not have wealth can easily acquire it. So let logic prevail; work with the market, go with its flow."

Mrs Blumkin drained her glass and refilled it herself. Ash became concerned.

"Once you have chosen your investments and settled on a workable routine, sit back and enjoy your youth, good health, your family, and the incredible planet you live on."

"But what should I invest in?" asked Ash.

The door opened and Juliet stepped in with Moses hot on her heels. Moses carried his silver tray with two empty glasses and a bottle of mineral water.

"Yes, Juliet?" said Mrs Blumkin.

"I thought Mr Ash's tea might be cold so I have brought some water."

"That's great," said Ash before Mrs Blumkin could intervene.

Moses approached the table, placed the tray on the table, and stepped back. Juliet then stepped forwards and filled both glasses, placing one in front of Mrs Blumkin.

Juliet and Moses then retreated. Once again, the door did not click shut.

Mrs Blumkin continued. "The best time to plant an oak tree is twenty years ago. The second best time to plant an oak tree is now. I recommend that you start investing now. To start, you don't have to invest a lot of money, but if you start now, it's so much easier than starting behind the game."

"But what should I invest in?" asked Ash again.

"There are many investment options to choose from," said Mrs Blumkin. "The trick is to pick the one that fits your life's ultimate goals."

Ash responded. "That means saving 10 percent of my income and investing it in an instrument that compounds and reinvesting the dividend."

Mrs Blumkin clapped her hands.

"You've got it, student Ash. That is what pay yourself first means."

Ash nodded. He did get it.

"Do this by stop order or direct debit. It will bring a lot of money, joy, and peace into your life. We have sourced an instrument that will not require you to be worried about how your shares are performing. Our strategy plans for a comfortable life and old age. This strategy will also liberate your children and their children."

Ash felt the burden lift from his shoulders.

"So that brings me to your question, 'what to invest in?'"

Ash had finally arrived at his Rubicon, and the anticipation was swallowing him.

"If a cross-section of industry is going to do well over time, then why waste your time and energy trying to pick the little gems? If you think you can do better than the market, I would advise you to look carefully. Very few people have the knowledge to be active investors, and this often includes brokers and fund managers."

Ash coughed as if he was choking.

"There are a few different investment avenues. You could go for the coffee shop investment, but its profits are not guaranteed and you might easily end up doing the work yourself. You could try a Ponzi scheme or emeralds from Thailand, but as you have learnt, this is not a great idea."

Ash laughed.

"You are looking for a vehicle that will offer 15 percent or more growth a year, where your principal is secure, that will pay a dividend and offers you the ability to compound your dividend, and you need this agreement to be legal."

"Yes," said Ash. The picture was becoming crystal clear.

"You could put your money into a savings account in the bank, but they will offer you a very modest interest rate. After you include inflation, you will find that you have lost money. Because of the low interest rates, the bank is not a candidate. Government bonds are secure, but they also offer conservative interest and your money is locked in for a certain period. And, if you choose to invest in the stock market on your own, picking the right shares is tricky. We discourage the average person from believing they can beat the market," said Mrs Blumkin.

Mrs Blumkin took yet another sip and sat further back in her chair.

"Risk is inextricably bound to the length of time you hold an asset. If you can hold an asset for years, you can afford to ignore the market's volatility. Ultimately, the needle of the compass always points back to ETFs."

Ash could sense he was close to ground zero.

"But first things first," exclaimed Mrs Blumkin. "Do you know what an index is?"

Ash shook his head. No. He had to be honest. He had no idea.

"There are many different companies listed on a stock exchange and many of these companies operate in similar fields, like mining, banking, energy, or retail sectors, for example. For convenience, the stock exchange groups these companies according to the sector they operate in, or they can be grouped according to their size. When these companies are grouped together, they form an 'index.'

"There are also world indices that include the world's largest companies regardless of where they are based. One such index is the S&P Global 100."

"Indices?" asked Ash.

"Yes," said Mrs Blumkin. "That is the plural form of index."

Ash was scratching his head. "Could you please explain what an index is again?"

"An index can be thought of as a basket of shares that includes a number of different companies. Some indices focus on a particular sector of the economy; others group companies according to their size. For example, the most famous index is the Dow Jones Industrial Average," said Mrs Blumkin. "It comprises of thirty companies listed on the New York Stock Exchange. In the United Kingdom, the FTSE 100 index, or informally called the footsie, comprises of 100 companies listed on the London Stock Exchange. In South Africa, we have the JSE All Share Index and the JSE Top 40. There are many different indices; some are industry- or sector-specific; others focus on the best-performing companies, and some focus on companies that are environmentally friendly."

Ash was catching on quickly.

"So, an index is made up of different companies and the weighted average price of all their shares is the index value," said Ash.

"Exactly," said Mrs Blumkin.

"Wouldn't it be great if I could buy shares in one index instead of buying shares in each company?" exclaimed Ash.

"That's exactly what an ETF is," said Mrs Blumkin. "It's a listed investment fund traded on a stock exchange, and it trades just like any other listed share. Just as you say, instead of buying one share in each company, when you buy an ETF, you are buying a share in all the companies listed in that ETF."

Ash got that.

"A listed ETF also gives you the opportunity to buy or sell whenever you like, just like any other share traded on the stock exchange."

"So, if there are forty companies forming an index, and you buy one share in that index, you are buying shares in all forty companies. Do you understand?"

"Yes," said Ash.

"So, if a few of those companies do badly, the rest pull the price of the share up. Do you understand?"

"Yes," said Ash, nodding enthusiastically.

"Why?" queried Mrs Blumkin.

"Because the share price of an ETF is based on the average price of all the shares in the index," answered Ash with a grin.

Mrs Blumkin was impressed and smiled at Ash. She had a good feeling about this student.

"Who owns an ETF, and how does it work?" asked Ash.

"Most ETFs are owned and listed by large financial institutions like banks. They are known as the ETF issuer."

Ash nodded.

"When this basket of shares, or ETF, gets listed on the stock exchange, it trades just like a share, which you can buy and sell, but it gives you the broadest possible diversification at the smallest possible cost."

"And this means I won't have all my eggs in one basket."

"Precisely," said Mrs Blumkin. "John Bogle, the man who created the first ETF forty years ago, was famous for saying, 'Forget trying to find the needle in the haystack, buy the haystack.'"

Ash didn't quite understand this.

"What he meant by this was why waste your time trying to find the little gems when you can buy the whole market."

Ash got it. Mrs Blumkin drained her glass, put it on the table, and picked up the glass of water.

"How do I buy an ETF?" asked Ash.

"You can buy shares in an ETF by placing an order with your stockbroker, online trading broker, or the ETF issuer," said Mrs Blumkin. "The beauty of an ETF is that the costs are limited."

Ash looked puzzled.

"When you buy into an ETF, you are buying one share in all the companies listed in that ETF, so instead of paying brokerage fees and commission on all the shares that make up the index, you only pay once, but you get a share in all companies forming part of the index. And there are no hidden costs or charges because the stockbroking firm or the online trading platform receives no commission other than the brokerage fees they charge for the ETF trade, and these fees have been negotiated and agreed upon upfront."

"Understood," said Ash. "That limits the cost of the middleman."

"Good student," said Mrs Blumkin.

"Are you taxed when you sell your ETF?" asked Ash.

"If a profit was made, yes," replied Mrs Blumkin. "But remember we advocate that you hold your ETFs for a very long period, but you will still be taxed."

Ash nodded, but he didn't like this. "Isn't the taxman being greedy?" asked Ash. "It sounds like the small investor is not being rewarded."

"The citizen's reward," said Mrs Blumkin, "is a stable economy and country."

Ash conceded the point and resolved to press ahead.

"What security does an ETF offer?" asked Ash.

"My, my," said Mrs Blumkin. "You have certainly grown."

"I am fortunate to have excellent tutors."

"I'll drink to that," said Mrs Blumkin, taking up her glass again. She raised it, but noticing it was empty, put it down and refilled it.

Ash raised his glass of water in salute and took a sip.

"ETFs tick all the right protection boxes," said Mrs Blumkin. "They are legal, you can sell or buy an ETF if and when you need to, your principal is returned to you when you sell, dividends are paid, you can reinvest your dividend, and, because an ETF is diversified, all your eggs are not in one basket."

Ash understood. His lights were coming on.

"The list of the good stuff goes on," said Mrs Blumkin. "An ETF is required to be fully transparent. This means that the ETF's performance is published every day. An ETF is also a safe place to invest because it is backed 100 percent by physical security."

"What is physical security?" asked Ash.

"Physical security is the share that you have bought. It is called 'physical' because it can be bought and sold at a price determined by the market."

"Does this mean I will get my money back when I sell my shares?" asked Ash.

"Yes."

The penny was dropping. Ash was close. He now understood how purchasing shares in an ETF made sense. It offered him much more security than anything he had previously heard or learnt about. He gave a small but enthusiastic laugh and decided to let the tax collectors have their "greedy" portion.

"Investing in an ETF is like crossing the street at a traffic light when the green man is flashing. It's safe and you don't have to bother about checking on the prices of your stocks because you know that in the long term the stock market will grow."

This worked for Ash. He was thrilled.

"So now that you understand how ETFs work, what index would you invest in?" challenged Mrs Blumkin.

Ash was unsure. He felt spoilt for choice.

"This is where conscious wealth comes to the fore. An index usually lists companies according to their size or sector, but some of these companies might have rapacious labour policies, others have an oversized carbon footprint, and others conduct business that is harmful to the environment."

Ash nodded.

"Conscious wealth is about investing in the future and not about cutting corners in pursuit of profit margins. The environment has borne this cost for too long, and it cannot sustain our narrow-minded profit incentive for much longer. We have to do more, and we can. Does this mean that you, the investor, will make less money? No, not at all. When the carbon tax is applied in the next couple of years, the cost to environmentally unfriendly business will rise, meaning the environmentally conscious company will have a head start."

The penny dropped. Ash got it. The lights went on. He sat on the couch looking at the floor, dazed.

"Conscious wealth is concerned with the pursuit of a higher purpose. Conscious wealth states that the way in which we generate profit must change if environment and businesses are going to survive," said Mrs Blumkin. "Conscious wealth seeks to invest in businesses with integrity and high environmental standards that serve all involved; that includes workers, suppliers, customers, investors, the community, and the environment.

"When companies invest in green technologies, their profit margins increase. We support fair trade, where suppliers of certain products have to fulfil certain minimum standards, such as sending their staff's children to school. For this reason, when you buy coffee with the fair trade label, you are paying more for it because the beans purchased have a real cost associated with their growing and harvesting. This does not mean that profit is negated; it means the real price is paid for the product.

"Like Mahatma Gandhi's policy of passive resistance, conscious wealth paves the way to a new brighter and sustainable future for democracy, capitalism, and the environment because it steers investment capital away from polluting companies to environmentally friendly companies without a confrontation. Instead of voting with your feet, you will now be voting with your wallet, and we all know money talks. This is the nonviolent change the world has been seeking. It's unstoppable!" enthused Mrs Blumkin.

Ash was staggered by the simplicity of the vision.

"If you stick to the rules," added Mrs Blumkin, "for twenty-five years and keep on investing your pay-yourself-first 10 percent, adjusted annually for inflation, and reinvest the dividend, your family will never be poor again. It's just the first few years that will be tough. After you have adjusted your living expenses and you grow your take-home pay, life will become easier. After twenty-five years, you and your progeny will be free. This is the return to the Garden of Eden."

Ash didn't understand.

"Before people started cultivating crops, they only worked for three or four hours a day and stress was unknown. These communities lived in harmony with the environment, and because they did not overexploit their food source, they didn't have to work very hard, and therefore had more than enough time for family, enjoyment, and spiritual matters."

Ash could not believe the magnitude of this simple truth; a return to the Garden of Eden with all the modern comforts.

"The secret remains the same: invest your monthly pay-yourself-first 10 percent in an ETF and reinvest the dividend. As time passes, sit back and enjoy your family and hobbies. Let the market and the compounding effect work for you. Our strategy rewards the long-term investor."

"How do I thank you?" asked Ash.

"You go out into the world," said Mrs Blumkin, "and start to live your life the way it was meant to be lived, and when the time is right, you become a mentor."

Ash ran his fingers through his hair. "Wow!"

Ash's journal entry 21.12. 2012

FREE AT LAST.

Mrs Blumkin, what a peach. Excellent! Green ETF… wow!

Investment profile:

Seek stock that grows by 15 percent per year or more.

Pays a dividend every three months.

No hidden costs.

Can recover your principal.

Offers the opportunity to reinvest dividend (compounding effect).

Invest for twenty-five-plus years.

Own as much of the stock exchange as you can for as long as possible.

Where to go from here? TK ahead.

CHAPTER 10
PAY IT FORWARD

Ash's journal entry 21.12.2015

Who would have thought such a simple idea could grow so quickly?

Here I am, sitting on my bed, the night before I fly to Chicago as keynote speaker at an international summit on conscious wealth. Whew! That's a long sentence. Whew! Who would have thought so much positive stuff could happen in three years?

When I look back, I can see how the Goddess was in charge of everything. She came to impart a message, and she delivered. High five! She has set us on a path to financial freedom. We will have earned it, no doubt, but so far the journey has been so positive.

Who would have thought that conscious wealth would be the Gandhi solution to capitalism? Such a simple solution; the individual invests in an index that tracks green companies. Brilliant. You are buying shares in the future and becoming wealthy at the same time. Instead of all the money flowing to unconscious companies, it now flows to environmentally conscious companies, in turn, forcing unconscious companies to change. Who would have thought? So simple!

Ash entered the Cape Town International Airport terminal building early because he liked being early. He found that when he left early, all the traffic lights were green for him and when he left late, they all seemed to be red, and because of this he found being early less stressful than chasing the clock.

Time had flown, as it does when one is having fun. The dark years had passed and he was once again enjoying days of abundance—Mr February's abundance, and more. Ash had left the hardware store and was now a management consultant. More grey hair had appeared on his head, his first daughter was going to school, and their home was nearly paid for. His love for Suraya had grown deeper; they were now a team and their family had welcomed another daughter. Confidence had returned to him, and once again, he and the wind ran as one.

He pushed his trolley to the check-in counter and completed the formalities before the maddening crowd arrived.

Once he had received his boarding pass, he headed to the newspaper stand and thought about buying something to read. The newspapers were full of bad news. Ash laughed; their business was selling advertising space, and bad news and disasters attracted readers. When he scanned the headlines, he felt a knot forming in his stomach, so he turned to the magazine rack. They also made their money by selling advertising space. That would not do. He scanned the book racks. No. Nothing caught his attention. He decided to get himself a coffee instead. He found a restaurant and took a seat at the window to see what life had in store for him while he waited for his flight to be called.

A young lady walked past him in a huff and sat at a table to his right. She dumped her bags on the floor, sat down, dropped her head into her hands, and began to weep, loud, guttural sobs that plucked at Ash's heartstrings.

When the waitress approached her, she managed to place an order for coffee and then scratched around in her purse for some coins. One fell on the floor and rolled away.

It rolled under the table and across the floor and made a wide arc, skirting between Ash's table and the wall. Then, like a meteorite being sucked forwards, the coin passed behind Ash and headed back out across the floor, but it did not return to its owner. Instead it made a smaller circle and headed back to Ash, where it started to dance round and round in ever-smaller circles. And as the circles got smaller, the coin danced faster and faster until, like a whirling dervish, it spun on its axis. Then it slowed and fell over.

"Well, I never," said Ash. "Who would have thought a coin could perform such a beautiful dance?"

Since he had conquered his fear of flying, Ash now loved planes. He found them graceful. But he still didn't like queues, so he waited until he was the last person to board. The cabin steward welcomed him and directed him to his seat. He waited while the other passengers stowed their bags in the overhead compartments and then proceeded to his seat.

Boarding last often means that there is no room in your overhead compartment, but Ash had that eventuality covered. He didn't carry hand luggage.

When he got to his seat, he found that the Goddess had been busy. The young lady who had been sobbing in the restaurant was sitting in his seat.

"I think you have the wrong chair, ma'am," Ash said gently.

She protested loudly.

Presently the air steward arrived and resolved the problem diplomatically. The young lady was indeed in the wrong seat. Hers was right next to Ash.

Once they were airborne, the Goddess got to work and prodded Ash into action.

"I couldn't help but notice your sadness," said Ash.

"Sorry. I tend to wear my heart on my sleeve." This was a fib, and Ash knew it.

"Can I help?"

"Thanks, but it's a bit too late."

"I am sorry to hear you say that," said Ash. "It's never too late."

Free at Last

About the Authors

Robert J Van Eyden

Robert Van Eyden is an academic who was appointed an associate professor of financial management at the early age of 24, teaching business economics, financial management, and investments. His PhD focussed on the application of neural networks and the forecasting of share prices. In 1995, his PhD thesis was published as book, entitled "The application of neural networks in the forecasting of share prices" by Finance & Technology.

Over his 20-year career in the financial markets, he has spent time as a quantitative analyst, fixed-income analyst, head of bond sales, global head of research, and the CEO of a stockbroking firm.

Respected for his business and personal skills, Robert is particularly noted for finding common-sense solutions to often complex problems. He actively participates in and is passionate about making the world in which he operates a better place to live.

P D Wells

P D Wells has enjoyed a rich and varied life. As an entrepreneur, his initiatives have included working as an art director for the movie industry and owning a café and theatre in Observatory, Cape Town, where he initiated a community magazine, festivals, and a park project. His social conscience and public spirit led him to adventures in Australia in health care and environmental issues, serving as artist-in-residence at a children's hospital and at Aboriginal centers. Peter holds a degree in fine art and a diploma in education and small business operation. He illustrated his first book, *Adventures in East Africa*, with his own watercolours. He has also written *Above Eden: A Journey to Enlightenment*.

For more information on *The Money Fountain* or the authors, please visit www.themoneyfountain. com or e-mail info@themoneyfountain.com.

www.ingramcontent.com/pod-product-compliance
Lightning Source LLC
Chambersburg PA
CBHW072024190526
45166CB00015B/483

* 9 7 8 1 4 9 2 8 1 2 0 9 8 *